Awakening the Sacred Flame: A Beginner's Guide to Kemetic Spirituality

Discover the Mysteries of Ancient Egypt for Spiritual Growth and Divine Alignment

Enlightened Editions

© **Copyright 2024 - All rights reserved.**

The content contained within this book may not be reproduced, duplicated or transmitted without direct written permission from the author or the publisher.

Under no circumstances will any blame or legal responsibility be held against the publisher, or author, for any damages, reparation, or monetary loss due to the information contained within this book, either directly or indirectly.

Legal Notice:

This book is copyright protected. It is only for personal use. You cannot amend, distribute, sell, use, quote or paraphrase any part, or the content within this book, without the consent of the author or publisher.

Disclaimer Notice:

Please note the information contained within this document is for educational and entertainment purposes only. All effort has been executed to present accurate, up to date, reliable, complete information. No warranties of any kind are declared or implied. Readers acknowledge that the author is not engaged in the rendering of legal, financial, medical or professional advice. The content within this book has been derived from various sources. Please consult a licensed professional before attempting any techniques outlined in this book.

By reading this document, the reader agrees that under no circumstances is the author responsible for any losses, direct or indirect, that are incurred as a result of the use of the information contained within this document, including, but not limited to, errors, omissions, or inaccuracies.

Contents

Introduction   3

1. Introducing Kemetic Spirituality   5
   Overview of Ancient Egyptian Civilization and Religion
   Kemetic Spirituality as a Contemporary Spirituality

2. Origins and Key Concepts of Kemetic Spirituality   12
   The Historical Background of Kemetic Spirituality and its Influences
   Key Concepts of Ma'at

3. Understanding Ma'at and Living in Alignment   17
   Truth
   Justice
   Harmony
   Order
   Compassion
   Wisdom
   Reciprocity

4. The Path of the Kemetic Practitioner   37
   Kemetic Practitioner Diversity
   Cultivating a Sacred Space
   Nurturing a Relationship With the Divine
   Cultivating a Relationship With Oneself
   Magic and Manifestation

5. Connecting with the Kemetic Pantheon — 59
   Importance of Living with the Netjeru: An Exploration of Divine Connection
   Key Deities in Kemetic Spirituality
   Connecting With the Pantheon
   Approach Practicing With Sincerity and Respect

6. Navigating the Path with Divination Tools — 83
   Intuition
   Oracle Cards
   Casting Lots
   Scrying
   Pendulum Dowsing
   Dream Interpretation
   Spiritual Hygiene Practices

7. Honoring Ancestors and Ancestral Practices — 97
   Establishing a Connection with Ancestral Lineage and Heritage
   Ancestral Veneration Rituals, Practices, and Offerings
   Prayers and Invocations
   Ancestral Healing and Reconciliation
   The Guidance and Wisdom of Ancestors
   Ancestral Veneration and Personal Growth

8. Sacred Texts and Wisdom of Egypt — 111
   The Funerary Texts
   Wisdom Literature, Proverbs, and Teachings
   Spiritual Insights and Guidance

9. Symbolism and Sacred Arts — 125
   The Role and Significance of Hieroglyphs
   Key Egyptian Symbols
   Use of Art to Convey the Divine and Create a Sacred Atmosphere
   Importance of Music and Dance in Religious Ceremonies

BONUS: Decoding the Language of Dreams — 142

Dream Interpretation in Ancient Egypt
Dream Interpretation For The Kemetic Practitioner
Common Symbolism For Kemetic Dream Interpretation
BONUS: Decoding the Language of Dreams (SPLIT)

Conclusion 161

Glossary 169

Further Reading 173
   Theology and Philosophy
   Literature
   History and Society
   Funerary Texts

References 175

FREE ENERGY HEALING MEDITATION

Are you ready to recalibrate your energy with the healing touch of goddess Isis?

As we journey through life there are many things that contribute to stagnant or blocked energy in our field. These blockages can lead us feeling depleted, disconnected, and disenchanted with life.

The Energy Healing Meditation, channeled by Katherine through her connection with goddess Isis, is a transformative journey into the sacred chambers of Isis's Philae temple.

This guided meditation serves as a tool for spiritual healing, facilitating a deep connection with the divine feminine energy embodied by Isis. Through the recalibration process, you may experience a realignment of your energy centers, fostering a sense of balance, clarity, and heightened spiritual awareness.

The meditation taps into the ancient wisdom encoded in the Philae Temple's sacred vibrations, infusing the energy recalibration with the potent healing frequencies associated with goddess Isis. Participants often report a sense of release from stagnant energies, emotional blockages, and even physical tension.

The energies harnessed here contribute to a spiritual journey that transcends time, providing contemporary seekers with a bridge to the sacred practices of ancient Kemetic spirituality.

Download your FREE Energy Healing Meditation by scanning the QR code below:

Introduction

"Seek peacefully, you will find." —Oracle at Siwa

Are you seeking spiritual guidance and a deeper connection with the divine in a chaotic world? Have you received the inner call from the Netjeru, guiding you to explore this path on a deeper level? At its core, Kemetic spirituality allows you to evolve as a human being. The Netjuru, closely aligned with our world, intentionally prioritizes your own spiritual growth and development and concerns themselves with allowing you to grow on this spiritual journey.

Right now, you might have a lot of questions that you need answered—and that is okay. One of the most important things to note is that everyone starts somewhere. At this point in your journey, you might be wondering what Kemetic spirituality is, as well as what makes up the core beliefs of it. You might be wondering how to connect with Kemetic spirituality and what you need to do to get there, as well as how to circumvent some of the challenges associated with working with ancient spirituality. All of this and more will be answered for you within the pages of this book.

Inside, you will discover the benefits of Kemetic spirituality in all aspects of your life. You will uncover how Kemetic spirituality can foster peace and personal growth, as well as a personal connection with the universe. Beyond that, you will find universal spiritual principles that help you unlock secrets to navigating modern life mindfully, all thanks to the power of spirituality. In addition, this book will empower you to understand how ancient Egyptian culture and concepts can deepen your divine connection and awaken your sacred flame within.

The sacred flame is a divine spark within each of us, as well as the eternal light connecting us to the Netjeru—the deities of ancient Egypt. It signifies transformative power and serves as a metaphor for the inner fire within each of us, the same fire that contributes to our passion for knowledge, wisdom, and understanding of the universe. It represents a desire to align ourselves with the principles of Ma'at, reminds us of the responsibility we have to honor our sacred path, and helps us maintain a connection to these powerful forces. Overall, the sacred flame is a symbol of divine presence. It is something within you and I as well.

It is a deeply personal and meaningful experience to be called to a spiritual path, as I experienced myself when the calling came from the Divine Mother Goddess Isis (Aset) through my dreams. I discovered this calling to be an invitation to explore the ancient wisdom and teachings of Kemetic spirituality, to embrace the divine feminine energy embodied by Isis, and to uncover the profound depths of my own spiritual potential.

Honor your own sacred flame and trust in the messages and guidance you receive, for they are whispers from the divine, guiding you toward a path of healing, growth, and connection. Embrace this calling with an open heart and a willingness to delve into the mysteries of ancient Egypt, for it is through this journey that you may find profound insights, personal empowerment, and a deep sense of purpose. May your path be illuminated by the presence and wisdom of the Netjeru, and may you discover the profound blessings and wisdom that await you on this sacred journey.

Chapter One

Introducing Kemetic Spirituality

"Just as a candle cannot burn without fire, men cannot live without a spiritual life." —Buddha

To be able to work with a thing in an adequate manner, you have to first be able to understand it. Spirituality is no different; you have to be able to understand the history, principles, and components of spiritual practice in order to work with it in a manner that is both effective and beneficial for you.

Kemetic spirituality finds its roots in ancient Egypt, with the term "Kemetic" derived from the ancient Egyptians' designation of their land as "Kemet", a term that directly translates to the "black land." This name stems from the fertile black soil deposited by the annual flooding of the Nile River along its banks. Thus, Kemetic spirituality refers to the spiritual and religious practices of the ancient Egyptian (Kemetic) civilization. It draws inspiration from the religious beliefs, rituals, and cosmology of ancient Egypt, which was one of the most advanced and enduring civilizations in the ancient world. It is essential to clarify that Kemetic spirituality is not a conventional religion but rather a holistic way of life. At its core, it centers on the pursuit of balance, inner peace, and harmonious living with oneself and the surrounding world.

The best way to begin with your Kemetic spiritual journey is by understanding the civilization that flourished along the Nile River. That is, understanding Egyptian culture will allow you to uncover the depths of Kemetic spirituality and value them for what they are. Moreover, this understanding will bring you insight as to how these practices are relevant to our modern life. From universal spiritual principles to personal sacred connections, exploring the background of Kemetic spirituality will allow you to unveil a path that is empowering—one that invites you to ignite your inner flame, embrace your divinity, and weave ancient wisdom into the tapestry of your existence. Let's dig in.

Overview of Ancient Egyptian Civilization and Religion

Even in ways that we cannot see, ancient Egyptian culture has been crucial to some of the modern developments that we enjoy today. From art to architecture, science to agriculture, and most notably for our purposes, religion, the ancient Egyptians made strides in their culture that have fundamentally altered the way that we interact with the world today. While you can dive into Kemetic spirituality without this background knowledge, I highly recommend taking the time to learn it now; not only will these benefit you when it comes to understanding the cultural context of the Netjeru and Egyptian religion, but it will make the learning process far easier on you. Let's take a peek into the structure of Egyptian society and some relevant aspects of the location's cultural history.

In general, it can be said that Egypt had a hierarchical society. When most people think of a hierarchical society, they think of stark contrasts between men and women, the rich and the poor, or something else. However, Egypt held a uniquely intricate hierarchical system compared to anywhere else on Earth. In Egypt, certain people were granted the title of Pharaoh. Pharaohs in Egypt were considered to be living gods, as if deities were walking our very own Earth.

Of course, they commanded significant amounts of respect and admiration. In Egypt, Pharaohs held total political and religious power. Rather than a world of politicians and priests, Pharaohs did it all—holding power in every aspect of society as it would seem.

These figures were revered due to the belief that they were intermediaries, allowing ancient Egyptians to have a go-between for the mortal realm and that of the divine. In other words, Pharaohs were respected due to their believed status as mediators between the gods and Earthlings. Many people were also under the impression that Pharaohs maintained cosmic order and ensured that a kingdom would prosper. It makes sense that they would experience a hierarchy based on the religious positions of Pharaohs within their society. Otherwise, hierarchy was more dependent upon a city, with nothing distinct to say about Egypt as a whole.

It is also notable that ancient Egypt was polytheistic, meaning that they worshipped more than one deity. For many people, especially in a society that emphasizes monotheism, acclimating to a polytheistic religion can be a bit frightening—after all, it is a bit more complicated than believing in just one deity. But fret not; the ancient Egyptians did it, and you can do it too. The group of deities that the Egyptians worshipped fell under the Kemetic pantheon, which refers to a group of deities belonging to a specific culture or practice. Each deity represented something different, with many falling into groups of nature, society, or characteristics. For practically anything you may think of, there was a deity to represent it that the ancient Egyptians worshipped.

One of the most important concepts to Egyptian spiritual practices—if not the most important—was the concept of Ma'at. Ma'at represented the universal balance and natural order, as well as truth and justice. As a central concept to Egyptian religion, Ma'at is something that you will become intimately familiar with as we progress throughout the course of this book. Much like certain principles are fundamental to Christianity, Judaism, or any other religion, Ma'at finds itself in the center of Kemetic spirituality. Many people, therefore, believe that Ma'at is the ultimate goal when it comes to spirituality.

Religious buildings also played a major role in the spiritual practices of ancient Egyptians. For example, where Western cultures have churches, ancient Egypt had temples. Temples served as Egypt's form of sacred spaces. Within them, people would provide offerings and perform rituals to honor whichever god or gods they worshipped—because many people did worship multiple gods, often having at least two. Within this religion, a male priest and a female priestess would play essential roles in the rituals, often leading or conducting them. Moreover, priests and priestesses would help others communicate with deities and perform religious ceremonies.

Ancient Egyptians believed in an afterlife as well—one where the soul continued its journey; for them, life did not end just because someone passed away. Funerals took place differently in Egypt than they do in modern, Western cultures as well. Many ancient Egyptians opted to work to preserve the body via a mummification process. Similar to how sentimental items may be placed inside of a coffin, bodies in Egypt were also provided with essential items to carry them through the afterlife. Namely, they were given a Book of the Dead, a collection of spells and rituals, and other items that would guide them through any dangers presented by the underworld. The hope of this was that it would equip the deceased with all they needed in order to obtain eternal life in the afterlife.

You should also be aware of the importance of symbolism in ancient Egyptian religion and art. For example, the Ankh symbolizes life, while the Eye of Horus serves as a symbol of protection. Various animals hold symbolic significance to Egyptian culture as well as hieroglyphs. As you navigate your spiritual journey, you may discover that many people wear these symbols—and others—due to their deep connection to them. This is something many people both in and outside of Egyptian spirituality do, believing that the symbols keep them safe and overall, spiritually connected.

Overall, it is important to understand the role that Egyptian culture and religion, as they stand in history, have played when it comes to how we interpret Kemetic spirituality today. Although Kemetic spirituality today and Kemetic spirituality in ancient times are a little bit different, we need to talk about what Kemetic spirituality today is like!

Kemetic Spirituality as a Contemporary Spirituality

Kemetic spirituality as we know it today closely mirrors that of ancient times in many ways. For one, it aligns with basic universal principles that have always been in tune with what the ancient Egyptians practiced. These principles transcend both time and culture, finding their way into spiritualities across the globe, new or old. Kemetic spirituality makes it a point to emphasize things like harmony, balance, truth, and interconnection, allowing those who practice it to find a footing in the universe as well as their place within it. It is quite a beautiful practice—one that helps many to find their purpose and reason.

One of the many reasons that people seem to flock toward Kemetic spirituality is because it is closely intertwined with these principles. If you think about today's culture and society, these are all things that are fundamentally lacking; capitalism and hustle culture, for example, do not really make room for truth, balance, and harmony. Seeking these things, things our souls naturally crave, many people turn to Kemetic spirituality. It is a spirituality that offers an approach that is both holistic and inclusive, being both a very open practice as well as one that benefits every area of life. In today's diverse and complex world, Kemetic spirituality anchors one firmly in principles of spirituality that simply feel good for us—because they are.

Kemetic spirituality also opens the doors to personal transformation and self-discovery in more ways than one. With its plentiful tools and practices, Kemetic spirituality as a spiritual path offers guidance that allows you to develop a full sense of who you are internally—one that does not rely on the world around you to tell you who you are. Additionally, Kemetic spirituality as spirituality offers the ability to foster inner peace. Inner peace is something that everyone can use more of in a society like today's, and the perfect way to find that is to delve into a spirituality that resonates with you. Moreover, Kemetic spirituality enables you to develop virtues like compassion and kindness, authenticity, and integrity.

As you seek inner peace and purpose, allow Kemetic spirituality to guide you. In its arms, you will find solace and the ability to empower yourself, heal, and self-reflect in a manner you have never experienced before. Kemetic spirituality is the most powerful tool—in my opinion—for deepening both your relationship with yourself and the world around you.

Beyond that, Kemetic spirituality enforces and encourages the integration of ancient and modern practices into one, creating a flourishing practice that allows you to remain in touch with all aspects of the cultural and spiritual world that birthed the belief system. Moreover, Kemetic spirituality involves addressing things that we face in our current world, whether it be on a personal or international level—it is truly a skill and a system that can revolutionize your life and the world around you. Principles of the Ma'at and their inclusion into our modern lives can align us with the greater good—what is most right in the universe. This can help us to navigate the modern world in a way that is both mindful and ethical, as well as in line with what we, as people, desire for ourselves and our future.

As you can tell, Kemetic spirituality is, despite having roots in very ancient practices, a phenomenal lens through which you can navigate the contemporary world. Besides what I've mentioned thus far, Kemetic spirituality puts a certain importance on the environment, allowing us to dive into how we can better the environment both personally and through environmental activism. Our environment is our home, and respect, fairness, and compassion in our interactions involve not just other people but our Earth and home as well. We need more people to be forward focused on the environment and activism in general, and Kemetic spirituality offers the opportunity to take a stand for that in a meaningful way. Kemetic spirituality inspires many to take steps toward equality and sustainability, influencing positive change in the world.

If you think that Kemetic spirituality is for you, I encourage you to let it guide you toward enlightenment, spiritual and personal growth, and a connection with the divine unlike any other. It is not something you'd come to regret.

Chapter Two

Origins and Key Concepts of Kemetic Spirituality

> *"Spirituality does not come from religion. It comes from our soul. No one is born with religion. Everyone is born with spirituality."*
> —Anthony Douglas Williams

In the last chapter, we discussed some of the contexts of Kemetic spirituality. Specifically, you learned a bit about the culture and history, as well as the role Kemetic spirituality plays in being a modern spirituality. Now, it is time to immerse yourself further, exploring the mystical depths of Kemetic spirituality and its sacred roots. During this chapter, you will uncover some of the guiding principles of Ma'at, including the profound presence of divine beings. You will discover the transformative power of sacred rituals and offerings and take a look at the intricate tapestry of symbolism holding keys to spiritual enlightenment. Through its powerful resurgence, Kemetic spirituality has offered modern practitioners a world of wonders. Let's explore it together.

The Historical Background of Kemetic Spirituality and its Influences

Understanding the historical background of Kemetic spirituality, as well as its influences, is important to understanding Kemetic spirituality as a whole. Over the course of thousands of years, Kemetic spirituality has evolved brilliantly. Most things fluctuate with time, and this beautiful spirituality is no different. As it has evolved, Kemetic spirituality has adapted and incorporated a world of new ideas and beliefs to match the changing culture around it. There are parts of Kemetic spirituality today that were not present at its inception, and that is nothing to shy away from, this spirituality welcomes change. Throughout different periods in Egyptian history, Kemetic spirituality has grown.

Let's go back to the roots of Kemetic spirituality. Kemetic spirituality takes its root in predynastic times, which occurred in roughly 3150 BCE and earlier. This was before typical recorded history existed, so most of what we have regarding this period in time is speculation and strong guesswork based on artifacts and evidence left behind by the people and time itself. During this period, the ancient Egyptians lived in a heavily agricultural society. Along with the agricultural development and time period that ruled history, ancient Egyptian communities worshipped deities connected to nature and fertility. This makes sense, as budding populations and the need for food have made this the most relevant aspect of life. It only tracks that these would be the predominant deities in the lives of the ancient Egyptians.

Eventually, centralization occurred in ancient Egypt. Cities were formed, basing themselves around central buildings and organizations. This led to the development of something resembling organized religious practices within Egypt. As I talked with you about earlier, Pharaohs became central, divine rulers within Egyptian society. At the same time, temples and other religious monuments were constructed in order to honor specific gods and goddesses.

For a while, this existed on its own, with just the influence of Egypt mattering when it came to cultural developments. After all, there were already so many new integrations, as it were, with the development of the city structure and the buildings that were being constructed. However, shortly after things began to settle within ancient Egypt, some new ideas began to intermingle with what already existed there. Neighboring cultures and foreign civilizations, over time, began to influence Egypt as well, leading to the assimilation of new practices and religious ideas.

Over millennia, the ancient civilization of Egypt developed a unique and profound spiritual belief system that was deeply interwoven into every facet of its society. Religion, with its rituals and practices, became an integral part of Egypt's daily life, and its influence was pervasive, shaping the culture, politics, and the very essence of Egyptian identity. However, what truly set Egyptian spirituality apart from other ancient cultures was its unparalleled emphasis on preparation rites for the afterlife. This distinctive focus on death and the afterlife led to the construction of grand tombs and the development of intricate burial rituals, most notably, the Book of the Dead.

The Egyptian civilization viewed life and death as interconnected stages of existence, where the earthly life was seen as a mere steppingstone to the eternal realm of the afterlife. This profound belief in an afterlife encouraged the Egyptians to devote significant attention and resources to preparing for the journey beyond death. Unlike many other ancient cultures, where the focus of religious practices was often centered around appeasing deities or ensuring a bountiful harvest, the Egyptians placed equal, if not greater, importance on the transition from the mortal realm to the eternal one.

The construction of grand tombs was one of the defining features of Egyptian spirituality. These tombs were not merely sepulchers for the dead but elaborate structures and monuments meant to safeguard the deceased on their passage to the afterlife. From the iconic pyramids to the rock-cut tombs in the Valley of the Kings, the grandeur and complexity of these burial sites demonstrated the

Egyptians' unwavering commitment to ensuring a prosperous journey for the departed.

Moreover, the development of burial rituals and texts, such as the Book of the Dead, showcased the sophistication of Egyptian religious thought and the belief in the continuity of existence beyond death. The Book of the Dead, a collection of magical spells and incantations, was intended to guide the deceased through the perilous journey of the afterlife, ensuring their safe passage to the realm of Osiris, the god of the dead. This sacred text was carefully inscribed on papyrus or linen and placed in the tomb, emphasizing the significance of its role in the afterlife journey.

The unfortunate news is that something caused the ruthless decline of Kemetic spirituality—the arrival of Christianity and Islam. These religions managed to wipe out much of the presence of Kemetic spirituality, making practitioners few and far between. But fortunately, there has been a recent revival in interest regarding Kemetic spirituality. People just like you are helping to revive this ancient spirituality with booming interest.

Key Concepts of Ma'at

Understanding the key concepts of Ma'at is something that is both a lifelong journey and essential to your understanding of Kemetic spirituality. The Ma'at represents one of the most significant aspects of Kemetic spirituality; it represents cosmic order and ethical conduct within spirituality, guiding us through life in the best of ways. It also represents the interconnectedness of all beings and each individual's unique role in contributing to the cosmic order and the overall well-being of the universe. Within Kemetic spirituality, many practices are considered to be integral, all of which we will discuss throughout the course of the book. Among the key principles and concepts are ancestor reverence, rituals, offerings, symbolism, and the use of sacred spaces.

Furthermore, Kemetic spirituality and Ma'at emphasize that all beings are interconnected not just amongst themselves but with the universe as well. The Kemetic pantheon of gods and goddesses is revered, with individual deities being invoked for particular guidance. As a part of Kemetic spirituality, spiritual transformation, and personal growth are sought after, with self-reflection and alignment with Ma'at being crucial to doing so.

As you explore this book, you will become intimately acquainted with each of these concepts and ideas. As we progress into the next chapter, you will uncover the main principles of Ma'at as well as their relevance to daily life in more depth.

Chapter Three

Understanding Ma'at and Living in Alignment

"The goal of life is to make your heartbeat match the beat of the universe, to match your nature with Nature." —Joseph Campbell

Understanding the principles of Ma'at is crucial to your Kemetic practice. The principles of Ma'at serve as a guiding light to ethical living, as they provide a framework for you to align yourself alongside the cosmic order. By embodying the principles of Ma'at, you have the power to cultivate a balanced and righteous existence. In the last chapter, we touched briefly on some of the key concepts that engender Ma'at and Kemetic spirituality as a whole. Now, let's take a deeper look into the core principles of Ma'at that you will need to know.

While the principles of Ma'at may vary slightly depending on the source, broadly speaking, there are seven principles that will serve you well—truth, justice, harmony, order, compassion, wisdom, and reciprocity. As we explore each of these principles, prepare yourself to encounter not just what they are, but how to embody the principles in everyday life as well. This will equip you with the skills that you need to embody Ma'at and live in justness and harmony with the cosmic order.

Truth

The first principle that you will need to know of is truth. Truth involves many things, but primarily it involves your ability to distinguish between what is real and what is not. Someone who is grounded in truth is going to seek and uphold truth in all aspects of life. While the truth is subjective to a certain degree, reality grounds itself in what is good and fair, including the belief that all creatures are sacred and deserve respect and honor. Someone who lives in alignment with the truth is not going to just seek out what's true and what's not—they will not act as a backseat driver when it comes to finding what's right and wrong in the world. Rather, someone who is aligned with truth will take the wheel for themselves, steering themselves into what is truly right and avoiding what is not.

Someone who embraces the truth is going to be an honest and sincere person. The mentality that lying is okay if it helps you out is not one that aligns with Ma'at. Rather, you have to be willing to have full transparency when it comes to your thoughts, words, and actions. This can be a rather difficult thing to do, especially if you are not used to living a life with truth as a central part of it. It is okay to recognize that you have to work toward something like this, understanding that there is going to be some hard work ahead of you to be truthful with yourself and those around you.

Part of embodying truth involves embodying integrity and avoiding deception and falsehood. While you can't control the actions of others, you can certainly control those of yourself. This means that you have a responsibility to pick and choose how you will behave. You can opt to deceive those around you, living a life guided by lies and falsehood—but if you do so, you will not be in alignment with Ma'at. On the other hand, you have the ability to make the decision to guide yourself using truth and integrity, making an active choice not to deceive others or engage in falsehoods. In fact, if someone ritualistically drags you into their own falsehoods and deceptions, a good step forward would be to cut them out of your life. As harsh as that sounds, we are only as good as the company that we keep.

Truth not only refers to objective truth and honesty in your interactions with others but also encompasses knowing and living by your own truth. It involves being true to yourself, understanding your own values, beliefs, and authentic nature, and aligning your actions with your inner essence. Living in harmony with your own truth is essential for personal growth, self-awareness, and spiritual development in Kemetic spirituality.

Becoming a more truthful person in the modern world can be hard, which is why I have some tips for you when it comes to embracing the truth. First, it is important that you are willing to have an open mindset that encourages curiosity and an open-minded attitude. You cannot embody truth if you allow your judgments and perceptions to be clouded by personal beliefs and biases. Rather, you have to be willing to open your eyes and see the world for what it actually is, letting truth into your life whether you like what it has to say or not. The truth is hard to digest, but no one said the road to excellence and alignment was easy!

Next, it is important to seek diverse perspectives and sources of information before you believe something in life. Everybody is going to believe something a little bit different from anyone else, and while we should embrace those differences, a true truth-seeker is going to want to hear as many diverse perspectives as possible. When you do seek out these differing opinions, listening with an open mind, you develop a stronger ability to discern the truth as well as to understand a topic with a higher degree of well-roundedness.

Critical thinking skills are also crucial when it comes to seeking the truth, because they allow you to evaluate evidence and arguments through an objective lens, one that is not clouded by your judgments and bias. This also includes changing your beliefs when your beliefs prove to be clouded or misguided, and being willing to challenge your beliefs is a sign of strength.

The way that you interact with others matters as well. When you talk to other people, it is important that you practice active listening rather than solely waiting on your turn to speak. Your dialogue should be respectful, and you should try your best to understand where they are coming from in a conversation. Part of seeking the truth is listening to what others have to say without judgment, even if their opinions differ from our own. In seeking the truth, you might find that you align with some of their beliefs as well as ones that you already hold. You cannot truly be a truth seeker if you exclude the opinions of some.

Moreover, you have to fact-check information before accepting that it is true. While opinions are just that—opinions—fact-based evidence should always be verified using credible sources, no matter how inconsequential that fact may be. Cross-referencing multiple independent sources is a phenomenal way to seek the truth when it comes to everyday life. You should also strive to embrace scientific methods and evidence, as well as overcome cognitive biases that can distort how you view the truth. One major cognitive bias is confirmation bias, wherein one seeks to verify that their opinion is true rather than trying to disprove it.

Finally, it is essential that you accept the truth as well as the knowledge that the truth can be uncomfortable or unsatisfying. Regardless of if you like the truth, part of alignment with Ma'at is accepting the truth anyway. Fostering intellectual humility—the recognition that our knowledge is limited and ever-changing—is essential as well, allowing you to update your knowledge base and perception of the truth as you navigate the world around you. Alignment with what's true is the first of many principles of Ma'at that you will need to be familiar with in your journey.

Justice

The next principle of Ma'at that you are going to need to embody throughout your journey is justice. Acting in accordance with justice means that you act in accordance with seeking equity for all people, cultures, and individuals on the planet. But what does it mean for there to be equity? Equity involves an equal opportunity for every living being to have their needs met, live peacefully, and meaningfully contribute to the good of society. This can apply equally to people and to animals, and someone who acts within justice will fight for equity and recognize its value in all areas of life. Embodying justice is crucial to alignment with Ma'at.

Those who embrace justice are people who act with fairness. They treat others and themselves fairly, making strides for what is right and pushing away at what is not. Integrity and righteousness are also valuable to someone who embodies justice. In all manners of life, someone who values justice will treat others equitably, ensuring that rights and dignity alike are respected. Impartiality is of the essence; this helps avoid biased treatment. This means that in order to behave with justice, you must be willing to treat people equally and with neutrality, even if they are not necessarily good people in your eyes.

Furthermore, you have to be willing to uphold fairness. Part of this involves making sure that those around you have equal opportunities and resources. This means that if you notice an injustice in your life, you will do what you can to combat it. Additionally, you will not make attempts to prevent justice from occurring when you have a choice in the matter. Upholding justice can be difficult at first, especially because we live in a world that can, at times, be rather cruel and difficult to manage. But to be in alignment with Ma'at, it is something that you need to work toward.

In order to embody justice, some skills that you can pick up include:

- Seeking education on the topic and principles involved in justice. This will allow you to better understand why justice is important and the practical implications of both justice and the lack thereof. This means understanding not just how justice exists and impacts you but understanding where injustice exists in the world and how it impacts others as well.

- Advocating for equal rights. Part of alignment with Ma'at involves making an active choice to fight for the equal rights and opportunities of everyone. Even if you do not resonate with their experiences or agree with who they are, regardless of background, race, gender, or sexuality, you should be willing to advocate for them on a personal level. This is part of making sure that each individual has access to equal opportunities and rights within our world.

- Supporting various organizations. Organizations and groups that fight for social justice and equality, especially when it comes to marginalized groups, are a valuable aspect of our society. In order to align yourself with concepts of justice, supporting these organizations financially, vocally, in protest, etc., is a wonderful way to get started.

- Engaging in conversation about justice. One of the most important ways that you can incorporate justice into your life is actually having conversations and discussions when it comes to justice. Furthermore, you should work to raise awareness and encourage both empathy and understanding within yourself and those around you. By doing so, you spread knowledge about the importance of justice as well as help others begin their journey with embracing justice.

- Encouraging inclusivity. In the place you work, go to school, or even the community around you, it is important to advocate for the value of diversity and inclusion alike. If you see someone being excluded, including them is only natural for someone who truly values justice. Moreover, someone who values justice will fight against systemic discrimination that is present at work or school, no matter how minute.

- Speaking up against injustice and discrimination. When you see injustice and discrimination in your everyday life, it is part of alignment with Ma'at to say something. Being an ally to people who are facing oppression or unfair treatment is only the right thing to do. Especially if you are someone of privilege, it is always the right thing to use that privilege to support others who are marginalized.

- Addressing systemic issues. While one person can only do so much, using your voice and your time to make a difference when it comes to addressing systemic issues that play a role in perpetuating inequality is a perfect way to work toward embracing justice. These efforts contribute toward a movement that brings us closer to a more just and equitable society, making it so that everyone can equally enjoy life with peace.

- Participating in peaceful protests and demonstrations. While many protests are violent, peace is also a major aspect of Ma'at. Using your time and energy to support peaceful demonstrations is a delightful way to make a difference because this helps bring lots of attention to injustice as well as advocate for change. By doing so, you help make the world a more equitable place for those who do not have the ability to speak up.

- Voting. One of the best ways that we can influence change—especially in the frame of justice and equity—is through using our voices to vote. If you are of voting age where you live, voting for leaders and policies alike that have it in their means to prioritize justice, fairness, and the protection of human rights makes a huge difference. Do not fall for the "your vote does not count" rhetoric—I assure you that it very much does.

- Reflecting on your own actions. Lastly, you can reflect on the actions and behaviors that you engage in. Make sure that you truly embody justice and treat others with both fairness and respect as you walk through life in order to truly align yourself with both justice and Ma'at.

As you navigate embracing justice and alignment with Ma'at through it, remember one important thing—do not just do these things for the personal benefit of alignment; rather, do them because you truly believe that they are the right thing to do. Alignment with justice will make the world a better place, but it is important that you truly understand the value of doing so in order to actually embrace it.

Harmony

Harmony is the third principle that you need to be familiar with in order to align yourself with Ma'at. Harmony refers to a state of being wherein all of the expressions of life—including you, humans, animals, plants, and more—are moving together in a way that is indicative of both alignment and beauty. Harmony involves an intricate balance both within and outside of yourself—one where you are balanced with Ma'at, yourself, and everything going on around you. In order to achieve harmony, every interaction and expression you set off must be authentic and full, expressing everything you are meant to. Authenticity is the key to harmony, which means that, above all, harmony is achieved by being true to yourself.

Someone who lives in harmony is someone who is willing to cultivate balance both internally and externally, meaning that balance in all areas of life is vital. Someone who seeks balance will ensure that they know themselves, navigate relationships with harmony, and are in balance with the world around them. Not only is it important to strive for internal balance, but you should also make sure that your actions contribute to the balance and alignment of the community around you, making everything around you more beautiful as a result.

Strive for equilibrium in all areas of your life and work to maintain a harmonious environment, and you are making good progress. Although, something like this is easier said than done. Here's how you can work to cultivate harmony and balance within your life:

- Practice both mindfulness and self-awareness. Mindfulness and self-awareness are gateway practices that take you directly to a place where you can understand your thoughts, feelings, and actions better. This, in turn, leads to a more harmonious embrace between you and the people and world around you—one where you are able to act within the scope of a balanced, beautiful synchronization.

- Practice gratitude and appreciation. Often, it is an easy endeavor to go about our lives without recognizing nor appreciating the positive aspects of life and the world around us. This is no way to live, especially if you hope to live in alignment with Ma'at. Instead, practice noticing things that you are grateful for every single day, and appreciating what you have, no matter how minimal that may be.

- Make sure that your lifestyle is balanced. While it may be tempting to work hard or spend a lot of time relaxing, all of this should be in balance. Work, rest, leisure, and meaningful relationships are all worthy of a dedicated spot within your life, and as such, it is important to ensure that you allow specific time to focus on each area in order to live in harmony.

- Make self-care and relaxation a priority. A lot of people come to spend so much time focusing on work and the world around them that they neglect to take care of themselves altogether. Part of harmony and balance is making time to take care of your mind, body, and soul—whatever that means for you as an individual. Without this transformative step, you cannot possibly be aligned with the concept of harmony.

- Resolve conflicts and disagreements well. Being able to resolve conflict and disagreement in a mature way is a skill that must be developed over time. Unfortunately, not everyone knows how to do so, which is up to you to determine if you know how. Managing conflict comes down to open communication and empathy, as well as the ability to compromise so that everyone is happy with an outcome.

- Maintain positive relationships. When it comes to the world around you, harmony is a big part of relationships too. This means that you should work to foster positive relationships with people around you—even people you do not know very well—so that you can promote a dialogue of understanding, respect, and cooperation amongst your peers. By doing so, you invite others to do the same and create a standard of respect that is unwavering.

- Embrace simplicity. Materialism and overconsumption are two things that can drastically throw off one's sense of balance. I highly recommend learning to embrace simplicity and even minimalism, learning to be happy without relying on material objects to create that for you. I find that the most purifying and rewarding happiness comes from within and blossoms only when materialism is let go. That doesn't mean that you shouldn't desire more for your life; rather, it means to be happy anyway in the unfolding of your desires.

- Spend time with nature. As humans, we are also a part of nature. This means that it is important to spend time with nature outside and learn to find a sense of calm and connection within it. If you live in a place that is safe to do so, walking through running water or bare foot on the grass can be impeccably restorative and help you develop a unique connection with the world around you.

- Set clear boundaries. It can be easy to let our boundaries waver and thus allow people to treat us any sort of way. But in order to have harmony with the world around you, it is essential to set clear boundaries in order to maintain personal control over what happens to you—as is your right. Making sure that others do not violate your boundaries is a good way to cultivate balance because it allows you to access the treatment you deserve.

- Practice moderation. Seeking the middle path—one that does not utilize extremes—will keep you in balance. This applies to every aspect of your life, including dietary consumption, spending habits, etc.

As you go about your journey with harmony and balance, you are going to need to continuously evaluate whether or not all aspects of your life are in harmony with one another. Overall, making sure that there is balance both inside and outside of yourself is essential to alignment with Ma'at. Make sure that you understand the value and implications of such harmony, doing what you can to balance all aspects of your life as you go.

Order

Order is the next principle of Ma'at. It involves the systematic and uncluttered arrangement of things in your life. Intrinsically, order necessitates that your life is free of excess and clear. Both your thoughts and actions should have a degree of organization to them, as this will align you more closely with Ma'at. Order is valuable because it keeps us calm, disciplined, and aware, and you should therefore seek to establish order in your personal life, as well as to contribute to the orderliness of society.

Someone who values order is not going to have excess belongings, nor will they live in a mess. They will not tolerate disorderly individuals surrounding them and will strive to help others attain order wherever they can. One way that you can emphasize order within your life is to create a daily routine. Divide your day into time periods that cover morning, afternoon, and night, and stick to that routine, including essential things like work and rest into your routine. This will ensure that you know what you are doing and when.

You should also make it a point to organize your space. Someone who lives in order cannot live in a space that is disorganized and cluttered. This means that you should take the time to declutter your home or bedroom, as well as to organize it in a logical way. Something important to keep in mind is that alignment with Ma'at is a constant journey. As such, you are not going to be organized overnight; it is something that you will have to steadily work toward as you become more in tune with your spirituality and purpose in life. Keeping things tidy is also good because it frees up your mind to focus on other, more essential tasks.

I also suggest creating a planning system for your life. Getting a planner—whether that be a virtual planner or a planner on paper—is a life-changing way to create order in your life. Create a system wherein you can manage tasks and responsibilities that you have to complete throughout the course of your day. Not only will this make you feel much more organized, but it will create order in the lives of those with whom you interact; people will not have to wait on you because you are late, nor will they come to view you as someone who is unreliable or disorderly.

In addition, you are going to need to develop time management skills. But what does time management have to do with order? Think about the last time you were in a rush, and this connection will quickly become apparent. Rushing and not having enough time for everything you need to do is overwhelmingly negative, causing disorder of all manners. But when you develop the self-discipline required to have strong time management skills, you are able to stay focused while simultaneously avoiding procrastination. This helps align you further with order and Ma'at.

Another characteristic of someone who has a strong alignment with order is the ability to find order even within the most chaotic of situations. For example, when in the midst of a rather complicated and disorderly task, someone aligned with the order will seek to simplify that problem, or they will break it down into a structured and manageable list of components. This is a wonderful mindset to get into because it allows you to transform immensely chaotic situations into ones that you can handle with ease.

Within relationships, you should also strive to maintain a degree of order. You can do so by practicing active listening and effective communication skills. What this will do is help you maintain order in your relationships, as well as help to avoid any potential misunderstandings—and we all know that misunderstandings within relationships so easily cause chaos.

Then, there's society. When it comes to personal actions that you can take in order to promote a fair and just society, it is rather simple—just work to embrace rules and regulations that are in support of a fair society that is in alignment with justice. Understand the importance of order for a functioning community as well. Now, not all laws and regulations are fair and just—including ones that are particularly discriminatory or perhaps have an ulterior agenda. These laws do not follow equity and just practices, meaning that they are excluded from order in a sense as well. Within an orderly life, do what you can to peacefully protest these occurrences.

Learning from past experiences, remaining adaptable, and regularly reviewing your progress toward goals are further steps that you can take in order to maintain order in your life. Remember that you are doing this for the betterment of yourself and the world around you—not solely for spiritual gain. I encourage you to resonate with and feel these strides deep within you.

Compassion

Next up, we have compassion. Compassion is a term you are probably familiar with—at least, I hope. Compassion involves showing empathy and kindness toward other people. It is a skill that everyone needs to have regardless of spiritual preferences, but it is especially important if you hope to be in alignment with Ma'at. Those who are compassionate are also empathetic, offering kindness and understanding toward other people in their daily lives. You should, as a part of being compassionate, also strive to extend understanding, generosity, and forgiveness in your interactions.

Compassion is not a hard skill to develop, but many people do not know where to start in cultivating it. In order to extend compassion toward others, you can:

- Practice self-compassion. Existing as a compassionate being begins with yourself. Therefore, it is important that you begin your journey into compassion by learning how to be kind and understanding to yourself because this sets the framework for being compassionate toward others. Treat yourself just like you'd treat a friend, acknowledging and embracing imperfections, rewarding yourself, and caring for yourself all the while.

- Cultivate empathy. Empathy involves a fundamental understanding of where someone else is coming from, which occurs through the process of understanding their feelings and experiences—even if they stem from something that you personally have never experienced. Someone who is empathetic gets along well with others, acting as a powerful mediator and friend alike. Along with this, it is important to learn how to put yourself in the shoes of other people, especially before you make a judgment or decision. This helps you consider their perspectives and needs before forming an opinion yourself.

- Engage in acts of kindness. Compassion, in theory, only goes so far; this means that you have to actually engage in actionable compassion. Treat others with kindness and generosity to engage fully with what it means to be compassionate toward other people, being selfless and kind as you do so.

- Do not hold grudges. It may be tempting to hold a grudge or even seek revenge, but this is not the path of compassion, nor is it a path that Ma'at encourages. Instead, strive to forgive others for their mistakes or wrongdoings. Remember that forgiving does not mean forgetting, and you can forgive someone while still holding them accountable in instances where they've genuinely wronged you.

- Volunteer. Volunteering and supporting charitable causes are a great example of how you can be compassionate in terms of your community. Typically, volunteer positions help those in need in some way, as well as extend to you an opportunity to give back to a community that you have undoubtedly benefitted from.

- Be patient and avoid comparisons. Part of being a compassionate human being understands that everyone has their unique sets of struggles and challenges, which inform their life in a different way than your experiences and struggles have informed yours. Furthermore, it is important to avoid comparing situations. While it is common for people to compare their struggles to see "who has it worse," this is not a compassionate approach. A compassionate approach is one that acknowledges the unique struggles that everyone faces.

- Speak carefully. When you talk, be sure that your words are kind and sensitive. Words can make a far greater difference than we think; be sure that you are speaking to others in a way that is mindful of how your words can impact them, and be grateful when others extend compassion toward you as well.

Compassionate actions are good for both others as well as yourself and bring you closer to Ma'at and what is divine.

Wisdom

The sixth principle of Ma'at is wisdom. For someone who is involved with Ma'at and aligned both with Ma'at and wisdom, seeking wisdom and knowledge is fundamental. Wisdom is a tool that we can use to navigate life's challenges and make informed decisions based on it. Knowledge and wisdom are crucial aspects of Ma'at; you have to cultivate a thirst for knowledge as well as self-improvement and the pursuit of higher truth in order to truly find yourself aligned with wisdom.

Everyone has the potential to find themselves closely entangled within wisdom, and you can do so by:

- Cultivate an open mind. Practice being curious and eager in everything you do, making yourself open to learning from various sources and experiences. Not only will this improve your journey as a spiritual practitioner by gifting you with knowledge from all walks of life, but this will align you with Ma'at more closely too. Remember the value of truth and harmony as well while you work on cultivating wisdom. Value what diverse perspectives have to offer—they grant us insight into the world in a novel manner.

- Use past experiences to your advantage. One of the best ways to embrace wisdom is to recognize our past experiences for the learning opportunities that they are. Our past experiences let us see where there's room to grow, which in turn gives us a springboard from which we can propel ourselves forward. Successes and failures alike provide us with valuable lessons, even if we do not understand how at the exact moment in which they are occurring.

- Embrace lifelong learning. Part of embracing wisdom is understanding how much you do not know and that accommodating that requires a lifetime of openness to learning that you have to be willing to maintain. This means that you have to remain engaged intellectually, seeking out constant opportunities for intellectual growth. To truly embody wisdom, you have to be willing to always seek to learn more, letting knowledge embrace you right back.

- Practice critical thinking and discernment. Many people hear about the value of critical thinking, but discernment can often be a new subject for people. Discernment involves being able to analyze and evaluate both information and sources critically, employing critical thinking and the quest for truth in determining if a source is reliable. This is vital to a quest for wisdom.

- See the big picture. You cannot truly be one who embraces wisdom if you do not have the ability to see the bigger picture and make considerations regarding long-term consequences before engaging in the decision-making process. Seeing the finer details is good, but being able to see how they work as cogs in the machine of a bigger picture is excellent.

- Know your own biases. Everyone has biases, whether conscious or not. Some of us allow our biases to impact us less than others, which is part of what it means to attain wisdom. In order to understand your own personal biases and how they inform you, practice both self-awareness and emotional intelligence, furthermore, spend time with practices like introspection and meditation in order to gain clarity and insight regarding your own thoughts.

- Share your wisdom with others. No matter what stage in your life and practice you are at, you have something unique to share with others. Do not be afraid to do so.

In addition, wisdom accompanies something called mindful awareness. You have to consciously be aware of your thoughts and feelings, aligning them with Ma'at at every opportunity. The quest for wisdom brings you one step closer to Ma'at, allowing you to know more about the world around you and what's right within it.

Reciprocity

And finally, we have the principle of reciprocity. Reciprocity is a concept that acknowledges that what goes around comes around. A rhythmic motion guides the world around us; cause and effect really take control and play a role in every aspect of creation. Reciprocity also involves the interconnection that exists between all beings, living and priorly living, and how actions have a reciprocal nature. To understand reciprocity, you have to understand that every action has an equal and opposite reaction, that everything is connected, and more.

Someone who engages with reciprocity treats others in accordance with the Golden Rule. That is, if you align with reciprocity, then you treat others how you would like to be treated. You foster positive relationships and mutual respect, understanding that what you put out into the universe is ultimately what the universe will give back to you. Ways that you can align yourself with and embody reciprocity include:

- Give and receive aid. Part of embracing reciprocity is being willing to give and receive both help and kindness when you interact with others. You can be the most selfless, giving individual in the world, but to truly be in alignment with reciprocity and Ma'at, you have to be willing to receive kindness and help in return. After all, if everyone is doing the giving and no one's receiving, who is there to help?

- Practice gratitude. There is no such thing as too much kindness. When someone takes the time out of their day to extend kindness or help to you, acknowledge what they've done for you and be grateful that they did so. The best way to return the favor in an instance like this is to then reciprocally offer kindness or help to someone else!

- Do not expect things in return. Part of embracing reciprocity is truly understanding that the good deeds that you will do will come back to you. Therefore, you need not expect things in return. Instead, look for opportunities to help others without looking for them to give you anything back. This fosters a spirit of generosity, building yourself and them up as you go. Even if they do not give you anything back, trust that they will give back in another way to someone else down the road.

- Express appreciation. It can be easy to let the kind things that people do for us pass us by. One of the best things that you can do to show that you value reciprocity is to express genuine thanks when someone does something kind for you, regardless of how big or small that act of kindness is. A simple "thank you" not only ensures that someone acknowledges their good deed, but it makes it more likely that they will continue to do kind things for others.

- Be responsive to others. When someone is in need of your advice or help in specific, listen attentively and actively, and actually help them out if you can. What this does is show that you value their needs, which is a step forward in indicating that you value them as a person. By making this stride, you create an atmosphere of mutual respect, community, and aid, which leads to my next point.

- Foster community. You can strive toward fostering a sense of community and mutual support by participating in community-based activities and helping out, when need be, when it comes to others in the community who are disadvantaged in some way. After all, if you were in their position, you'd hope for someone to help you out.

- Be a reliable, trustworthy individual. When you promise someone that you will do something or make a commitment to them, ensure that you actually follow through with that behavior. In that way, you can encourage others to reciprocate trust.

- Do not take advantage of others. Part of reciprocity is actually giving back, and that means avoiding taking advantage of the kindness or generosity of others as well as being mindful enough to create a balanced and respectful exchange.

One of the most important things that I can stress to you about reciprocity is to understand that reciprocity is not always immediate. You are not going to magically receive an equal and opposite gift for extending something kind toward someone else, and expecting that you will is not in the spirit of true reciprocity. Rather, you should be patient and wait for opportunities—both to give and receive. Doing so will align you more closely with the principles of Ma'at.

These seven principles come together to form the foundation of aligning yourself with Ma'at and what's good in the world. With mindful awareness of how you think, feel, and behave, you can work with all seven principles of Ma'at in order to align yourself more closely with it. By embracing Ma'at, you embark upon a transformative journey toward a life of purpose, integrity, and balance, contributing to the development of a more harmonious and just world.

Chapter Four

The Path of the Kemetic Practitioner

"The spiritual journey is individual, highly personal. It can't be organized or regulated. It isn't true that everyone should follow one path. Listen to your own truth." —Ram Dass

The path of the Kemetic practitioner is one that involves cultivating a close relationship with the Netjeru—the deities of ancient Egypt—as well as living in harmony with Ma'at and embracing the power of magic and manifestation. In this chapter, you will be guided through exploring the diverse nature of Kemetic practitioners. Alongside that, you will gain insight into how you can create a sacred space, cultivate a relationship with the divine, come to know yourself and harness the energy of magic.

It's important to recognize here that although I may suggest different paths for the Kemetic practitioner, the spiritual journey is personal and uniquely yours; everyone's path is different, shaped by your own individual experiences and connections with the divine. Within you lies your own vast wisdom, use this book as a guide, but trust your own guidance and intuition as you navigate your unique spiritual journey.

Kemetic Practitioner Diversity

There are many different forms of Kemetic practitioners, as it is a diverse religious and spiritual belief that welcomes people from all walks of life. Understanding the diversity among practitioners will help you not only understand the history and structure of Kemetic spirituality, but it will help you understand where you stand within the spirituality as well. Furthermore, it is important to note that the individual paths and approaches that people take reflect the kinds of people who embrace them. You can closely observe practitioner diversity by taking a look at the different categories of practitioners who embrace this spirituality.

Independent and Solitary Practitioners

Independent and solitary practitioners are just what they sound like—people who choose to explore Kemetic spirituality and all that it has to offer without the support of a formal group or organization. Many people wrongly believe that in order to practice Kemetic spirituality and similar spiritualities, you have to belong to a special group or organization. This is not true at all; you can be a solitary practitioner, which is just as valid as practicing among a group or from the inside of an organization. In fact, independent and solitary practitioners feel valued and inspired by the freedom that they have as a result of flying solo because this allows them the opportunity to tailor their practice to suit their unique spiritual journey and needs.

Most people who take the approach of an independent or solitary practitioner tend to engage in things like personal rituals, studying ancient texts, and seeking spiritual growth through a more self-guided approach. It is hard to put a specific definition to just what it is that individual practitioners do, which is due to the very nature of practicing independently. That is, it is so freeing and customizable that you can do virtually anything within the scope of your particular practice—which is a major reason why people opt to always remain solitary practitioners! However, if you are not interested in practicing solo, there are other options for you.

Group Worshippers

Another equally popular method of embracing Kemetic spirituality involves group worship. Group practitioners are on the exact opposite end of the spectrum from individual practitioners. Group worshippers tend to find solace and connection within communal worship and gatherings. Practitioners who opt for a group structure join together in formal groups, sometimes called circles or even covens, and often join within temples. During these meetings, practitioners are known for sharing rituals, traditions, and knowledge. It is not uncommon for group worshippers to find strength and inspiration in the collective energy that is present within a group setting; it is an opportunity to foster a sense of community and support among like-minded individuals.

Typically, group worshippers belong to more formal groups that vet their members through an application or initiation process. Due to laws regarding religious and spiritual teachings in many countries, these groups are only open to those of legal age within a given location. If you are of legal age and interested in seeking what type of groups are in your area, give a quick internet search to "Kemetic covens near me," "Kemetic circles near me," or "Kemetic spirituality near me," and you may find something. You can also use Facebook, Reddit, and other social media sites to help yourself network with other Kemetic practitioners both locally and online!

Afro-centric and Wiccan Practitioners

Afro-centric and Wiccan practitioners are another group of practitioners to be aware of. Egypt is an African country, and as a result, some Kemetic practitioners opt to emphasize the African-centric elements of the Kemetic tradition. This involves efforts to reconnect with the African roots that fundamentally make up Kemetic spirituality. Someone who practices Afro-centric Kemetic spirituality is going to potentially incorporate a wide array of African aspects in their practice, including but not limited to culture, history, and symbolism. This is a part of keeping the initial and traditional ways of Kemetic spirituality alive, inspiring other practitioners to embrace the African roots from which Kemetic spirituality blossomed.

Wiccan practitioners exist as well. Now, Wicca is in and of itself its own religion, which comes along with its own codes, rules, and beliefs. Some Wiccans opt to integrate elements of Kemetic spirituality into their practice, and others opt to do the exact opposite, primarily practicing Kemetic spirituality but incorporating elements of Wicca within their practice. This is a beautiful way that some practitioners blend Kemetic spirituality with modern and neo-pagan practices, creating an idiosyncratic and eclectic spiritual path unlike any other. While most Wiccan Kemetics tend to be solitary, there are some groups that dedicate themselves to this line of practice.

Reconstructionists

Next up, we have reconstructionists. Reconstructionists are individuals whose practice closely adheres to reconstructed practices. In other words, reconstructionists are dedicated to the art of studying and reconstructing—or rebuilding—ancient Kemetic practices as faithfully as possible. The aim of reconstruction is to study historical evidence and archaeological findings in order to practice the religion as closely today as it was practiced at its inception. A glorious path to tackle, reconstructionists spend their spiritual journey keeping alive practices that otherwise might've been lost to time as a result of its passage.

As a part of the practice of reconstructionists, they strive to revive the ancient rituals, ceremonies, and beliefs that were active when Kemetic spirituality was popular within ancient Egypt. This also involves a close adherence to the wisdom presented by the ancient Egyptians, in some cases involving ancestor veneration if one has a personal connection to Egyptian history—although, this is not necessary to be a Kemetic reconstructionist. In all, Kemetic reconstructionism involves an approach that is heavy on extensive research and a deep understanding of ancient texts and artifacts, making it a practice that truly is not for the weak.

Reformed Practitioners

The last group that we have are reformed practitioners, which in essence are practitioners who take ancient Kemetic spirituality and reform—or adapt—Kemetic spirituality to fit within the scope of a modern practice. Reformed practitioners represent a group of Kemetic practitioners who adapt the spiritual traditions of Kemetic spirituality to a modern lifestyle, while simultaneously maintaining the core principles involved. In a sense, reformed practice is the opposite of reconstructed practice. While reconstruction seeks to preserve ancient Practice, reform seeks to adapt ancient ways to modern times. Though, this does not mean that reform practitioners let go of the Netjeru, Ma'at, or other core principles.

Rather, reform practitioners interpret ancient teachings in a way that resonates with contemporary logic and practices, allowing for the traditions of Kemetic spirituality to evolve in order to remain relevant to modern times. Often, reform Kemetic believers will adapt and integrate insights from various sources, as well as work to apply Kemetic spirituality to their personal growth, principles of ethical living, and spiritual exploration.

The richness of Kemetic spirituality is only furthered by the diverse perspectives and approaches that practitioners of the spirituality embrace. Regardless of what approach one takes, each path available represents an idiosyncratic journey toward understanding the ancient wisdom and divine knowledge of ancient Egypt.

Cultivating a Sacred Space

One of the first things that every practitioner needs to do in order to embark upon their journey is to set themselves up in a sacred space. A sacred space is going to be the place in which you predominantly practice, one where your spiritual items and protections hover. For many people, their sacred space is private, while others choose to create one out in the open. The choice is yours, but in order to do so, you have to know how. Let's take a look at how you can cultivate a sacred space of your very own.

Creating an Altar

In short, an altar is going to be a sacred space where your tools sit, as well as where you convene for spiritual practices like rituals, prayers, offerings, and more. Not every practitioner has an altar, but I find that it gives you a place wherein you can center your craft if you do have an altar that is clearly laid out. But how do you go about doing that?

The first thing that you need to do is to select a dedicated space. Some practitioners opt to have more than one altar, but it is always good to start small when beginning anything new. Therefore, let's just start with one altar: your main altar. You can opt for an area indoors or out of doors, picking a place that feels good to you. You can use a table, shelf, windowsill, cabinet, or any other flat surface that calls to you. Because a lot of practitioners work with the elements, I recommend finding a spot where you are near a window and have good ventilation if possible. But some practitioners begin by working out of a shoe box—yes, a literal shoe box—so do not worry about your space being picture-perfect at first. There's always room to grow later.

Next, you are going to physically clean your space. You want to build an altar on a clean surface and in an area that is free from clutter. I recommend starting with a blank slate by removing everything from the surface that you plan to use as an altar. Then, with an appropriate cleaner, wipe down the surface and ensure that it is as pristine as possible. You should keep in mind that an altar is sacred and should therefore be treated as such, which means you do not want any common household items (water bottles, food, trash, etc.) to clutter it. Take everything off of your altar before setting it up if you can.

Then, you are going to start assembling, which is the most fun part. At a minimum, you are going to need something to represent each element. For example, a candle for fire, a feather for air, a cup or bowl for water, and a crystal or rock for earth. This is a very basic setup that many practitioners begin with, which is also accessible if buying supplies is not within your means right now. Beyond that, it is up to you what you put on your altar, though everything should have purpose or meaning. Choose items for your altar that resonate with your spiritual practice. Some ideas you can include are candles, crystals, statues for deities, offering materials, books or resources related to the craft, sacred symbols, and nature-based elements like flowers.

Arrange the items on your altar with intention, making sure that you do not just toss everything together haphazardly. Your altar should be arranged with care, and the symbolism and energy of each item should be kept in mind. However, remember that there's not really a "wrong" way to assemble an altar either—just do so in a way that feels harmonious to you!

Cleansing a Space

Cleansing your sacred space is the next aspect of cultivating a sacred space. Cleansing a space involves removing the existing energies—usually bad, but sometimes this can include both bad and good energies—in order to purify a space. I recommend cleansing before you set up your altar, as well as cleansing before any major spell or ritual. Furthermore, if you plan to practice anywhere other than your altar, absolutely cleanse that space as well. When it comes to cleansing a space, there are several different methods of doing so, which means that at least one will be able to work for you.

The first method that I always recommend for cleansing is a salt cleanse, although this method should be avoided if your altar is situated outside—sprinkling salt into the soil can be a very bad thing for the environment, preventing plants from growing and even killing existing ones, which is not in alignment with what we stand for. If your altar is outside, I recommend substituting other environmentally safe methods for cleansing. But for indoor altars, salt can work well. Simply sprinkle your salt on top of or around the perimeter of your altar in order to purify and cleanse the space. It is believed that this works because salt can absorb negative energies, which makes salt a great cleansing candidate if you are hoping to only cleanse negative energies.

Sound is another excellent method for cleansing a space that can work indoors and outdoors, and it is especially accessible to those without resources or many materials. Some ways you can use the power of sound to cleanse a space include: ringing a bell, playing a singing bowl, sounding a gong, using a chime, beating a drum, shaking a rattle, or even using your voice in the form of mantras or chanting. The vibrations of the sound help to dispel stagnant energy, replacing it with fresh energy that is lighter and uplifting.

Incense works well, too, if you are someone who favors smoke or incense as a cleansing method. It is a common method used to purify a space and can be used to make a space feel far more sacred, too. There is no hard rule for how you have to select incense for cleansing; pick a scent and type that resonates with you and carry it as you walk around the area, allowing smoke to waft by. You can similarly use cleansing herbs like cedar, sage, or palo santo to clear the space, which usually comes in herb bundles that can be ignited.

As you cleanse, do not make the basic rookie mistake of forgetting doors, corners, windows, the floor, and the ceiling. Make sure the whole area is cleansed. Ultimately, it is up to you which method you select for your cleansing needs. Pick one that works best for your circumstances and have at it!

Establishing Boundaries

The next step in developing a space for yourself that is truly sacred is to set boundaries, both internal and external. Start by setting an intention for your altar. Your intention does not have to be super specific, but it can be if you have a designated purpose for your altar. For instance, if you set up an altar with the explicit intention of working with deities, then you can use that for your intention. However, if your intention is just for the altar to be a sacred space in which you can practice Kemetic spirituality and magic, that is a sound intention as well. Set your intention either mentally or verbally. Then, either meditate, pray, or connect to divine energies—which we will discuss soon—in order to cement that intention.

Once you have done that, it is important to set external boundaries as well. If you live with other people and have the ability to do so, it is a good idea to set boundaries for your altar. You can do so by letting others in your household know to respect the boundaries of your sacred space, as well as letting them know that it is a place of reverence. If someone disrespects your space, open a kind and informative dialogue about it, letting them know that regardless of their reason, it is never okay to violate someone's personal boundaries.

Self-Purification and Ritual Baths

We've talked in depth about cleansing and preparing your space, but what about cleansing yourself and your body before engaging in sacred tasks? I recommend engaging in a self-purification ritual or a ritual bath—both of which are incredibly accessible to beginners—prior to engaging in any spell work or other spiritual endeavors that are sacred in nature.

Ritual baths are a great way to both soothe yourself and cleanse yourself physically and spiritually. Now, you do not have to engage in a ritual bath every time you do something involving Kemetic spirituality or your altar, but before larger works or acts of devotion, it is definitely a good idea. You can take a bath with added herbs, essential oils, Epsom salts, or other ingredients to your bath. If you are interested in finding out in specific which herbs are good for a cleansing ritual bath, research "herbal correspondences cleansing," and you will find everything you need.

Mindful cleansing can also be a helpful tactic for beginning your process. Before you enter your sacred space or begin your work, take a moment to breathe mindfully. Pay attention to where in your body you feel the breath enter and exit, as well as how it feels to breathe in and out generally. Then, set the intention to yourself to leave any worries or negativity outside of the sacred area. This will ensure that your sacred space and workings are not interfered with.

The last step that I recommend for this process is to engage in a grounding and centering meditation. Grounding connects you to the energies of the earth while centering ensures that your focus is directed toward exactly what you are working on. You can do so by following a guided meditation online, then eventually developing your own practice for grounding and centering.

Nurturing a Relationship With the Divine

Of course, your spiritual journey cannot really get off to a good start unless you truly work toward nurturing a relationship with the divine. The divine includes the Netjeru, which is the pantheon of Egyptian gods and goddesses that Kemetic practitioners worship worldwide. And why do you want or need to form a relationship with the Netjeru? Well, not only is it a fundamental aspect of Kemetic spirituality, but the Netjeru have a fundamental relationship with humanity—one that is mutually beneficial. In essence, the Netjeru help human beings like you and me grow and evolve in accordance with their guidance, and in return, they receive our worship and devotion, much like in any other religion. It is quite a beautiful thing.

It is important that you remember the principle of reciprocity when it comes to working with the Netjeru. Unlike in some other religions, the relationship between you and the Netjeru is meant to be a reciprocal transaction, not one guided by luck or fear. Fundamentally, worship energizes the Netjeru, providing them with the strength and power that they need to continue doing what they do best including helping us. By maintaining a reciprocal relationship with the Netjeru, you foster this reciprocal relationship that, in turn, helps advance your growth. In turn, that growth builds momentum that can incite positive change in the world around us. It is a chain reaction that keeps on giving, starting with just one practitioner like yourself. Your individual worship contributes to the Netjeru's ability to continue providing for us as a society and you as an individual.

I spent a lot of time discussing Ma'at with you earlier, and there is a good reason for that. Working in alignment with Ma'at and principles of ethical conduct is vital to your journey as a spiritual practitioner. All religions have rules, and you can perceive Ma'at and ethics as rules by which to abide during your lifelong journey with Kemetic spirituality. The Netjeru are not going to strike you down or anything like that, but more favor is shown to those who truly align themselves with these concepts and beliefs because these surround what the Netjeru themselves stand for.

There are hundreds of Kemetic deities, and while you can technically work with the pantheon as a whole, you are not going to have a deep, fulfilling practice if you try to form a personal bond with every single Kemetic god or goddess. Part of your journey involves selecting a few—or even just one or two—deities with whom you plan to build a personal relationship. This relationship will be based on resonance and guidance. At first, it might be hard to decipher which deity or deities you resonate with the most. Sometimes, signs will appear, or deities will come forward themselves, indicating that they hope to work with you as a part of your path, as Goddess Isis (Aset) did for me when she called to me in my dreams. If this does happen, you do not have to feel obligated to work with whoever comes forward; it is a decision you can make, and they will understand a polite decline.

> *"The problem of human existence is the forgetfulness of the Divine essence of the Self and the identification with the body as the Self."*
> ~ *Egyptian Book of the Dead*

It is also important to keep in mind concepts of interconnectedness as you work with Netjeru. A lot of people regard deities as some otherworldly beings who are inaccessible or somehow "better" than we are, but that is not at all the case with the Netjeru, nor is it how they wish to be interpreted. Rather, it is best to understand that deities are not separate from Earth or from us as humans because we are all interconnected. Moreover, the relationship that we have with divinity is one that already exists, which should soothe your worries anytime you feel like you are doing something poorly. In fact, according to the Kemetic belief system, every living being is part divine, thus the divine connection is always there, within and without, and by making the active decision to work with Kemetic spirituality and the Netjeru, you are simply acknowledging that bond.

As you work with the Netjeru, develop an attitude of compassion and trust. Trust that the Netjeru will guide you where you need to go and that they will never misguide you. Everything does happen for a reason, and if the Netjeru offers a piece of guidance that does not make sense, trust that it will when the time is right. Always remember that you are not alone, but you also cannot rely solely on books and information; you must cultivate and use your intuition as well.

It is also important to keep in mind that Kemetic spirituality is not a cerebral experience; it is a mystical experience. While knowledge is power, experience is empowerment.

Cultivating a Relationship With Oneself

> *"Within you there is a stillness and sanctuary where you can retreat at any time and be yourself"* ~ Hermann Hesse

Cultivating a relationship with yourself is something that takes a significant amount of time, but it is definitely worthwhile. In order for any relationship to be stable, nurturing, and fulfilling, you have to be willing to know yourself and give certain parts of yourself to the relationship. You have to be able to share who you are with those around you in order to truly cultivate a relationship that matters, and in order to do so, you must first know yourself. Knowing yourself can be a difficult thing, especially if you feel like you do not currently know anything about yourself—which is okay, as many people start from this place. But there's no way around it; to have a solid relationship not just with people on Earth but with the Netjeru as well, you have to know yourself. Plus, this aligns with the first principle of Ma'at—truth.

Do not worry about how long it will take to know yourself. The Netjeru realize that it can take some time for humans to get to know themselves because, after all, we are humans for a reason. Depending on your beliefs, this is your first time on Earth in this form as well (or at least the first time you can remember), making it even harder for you to navigate what life throws your way. Furthermore, do not feel like you have to know yourself completely to begin your spiritual journey. You are never going to feel like you know enough, connect enough, or are enough if you set the standard of waiting to begin until you hit "enough." Therefore, it is a good idea to jump right in and allow your spiritual relationship to flourish alongside your relationship with yourself.

To build an authentic connection with those around you, you must know yourself, and that includes your strengths, weaknesses, values, and aspirations. By knowing these things, you will be able to share yourself genuinely with others. This is further enhanced when you throw self-awareness into the mix. Plus, self-awareness can enable us to extend both empathy and compassion toward others while simultaneously making room for us to understand our own struggles and relate them to the struggles of others.

Furthermore, you must also know yourself in both physical and non-physical aspects. Cultivating a relationship with yourself means that you have to understand your physical body—including how it works, how you feel about it, and more. But not only that, but you also have to pay attention to how you feel, think, and interact with the spiritual world. Holistic self-awareness fosters inner balance and harmony, which not only contributes to overall well-being but allows you to dive into spirituality and your relationships with your deities as well.

Finally, grounding is an important practice for deepening your spiritual connection. Grounding anchors your physical body to the Earth, allowing you to draw on the Earth's energy and stability while remaining connected to the spiritual world. When you are grounded, you can maintain a deeper connection with your higher self and spiritual beings while simultaneously maintaining a sense of presence and stability in your physical existence.

How to Connect With Yourself

Meditation

The first practice that you can work with in order to allow you to get to know yourself is meditation, which is beneficial for clearing your mind. The best thing to do is to develop a regular meditation practice, which involves meditating every single day, even if it is just for a few minutes. Most people find that it takes around three weeks for meditation to "kick in." In other words, it takes about three weeks for you to begin to notice the positive effects of meditation, but once you do notice those benefits, it is a lovely state to be in.

Regular meditation allows you to clear your mind, release mental clutter, and cultivate inner peace and clarity. This helps you connect with yourself better because you are not so worried about extraneous things. You are not worried about stress, what happened the day before, drama, and more. Instead, during meditation, you have the ability to objectively consider your thoughts without judgment in a way that is productive. Moreover, meditation helps you become present, aware, and mindful of your thoughts and emotions alike. Not only is this good for your personal growth, but it is beneficial for your spiritual growth as well because you are able to actually focus on the spiritual endeavors in which you are engaged.

If you're new to meditation, I recommend picking up a steady meditation practice by finding five to ten-minute guided meditations online and following their guidance, picking a few that you like to return to over and over. Once you have mastered shorter meditations, you can move on to longer ones that are about half an hour. Some people even meditate for eight hours at a time—how incredible! If you're up for it, you will ideally move to silent meditation or mantra meditation, as these are more conducive to exploration of your inner world without external guidance.

If you feel ready to embark on a silent meditation practice, as is my preferred practice, one valuable piece of advice I will leave you with is that the goal of silent meditation is not necessarily to remove all thoughts—because that is a very challenging goal to achieve—but rather to cultivate a certain quality of awareness and presence. In many meditation practices, the emphasis is on observing thoughts without becoming attached to them or being carried away by them, allowing them to flow in and out of your mind effortlessly. The aim is to develop mindfulness, which involves being fully present in the current moment and accepting thoughts as they come, without judgment.

Breathwork

The next thing that you can do is engage with breathwork, which involves controlled breathing. Breathwork is useful for calming your body and your mind, helping you become more present. Breathwork includes exercises like deep breathing, pranayama, and other breathing exercises. These exercises are beneficial because they allow you to release both physical and emotional tension, clearing blockages that then allow you to become more in tune with your body and your emotions. It is also important to bear in mind that something can be said for conscious breathing. That is, conscious breathing, wherein you pay attention to each individual inhale and exhale, can allow you to center yourself and connect to your inner essence.

There are hundreds of breathwork exercises you can engage with. For example, I recommend breathing exercises for relaxation, as some of these are my favorites. One of my favorites is the 4-7-8 breathing method. This method involves inhaling for four seconds, holding your breath for seven seconds, and then exhaling over the duration of eight seconds. This exercise is both mindful and helps soothe the nervous system, providing you with all-around positive benefits.

Offerings

The next way that you can get to know yourself is to make offerings to the Netjeru—either individual deities or the pantheon as a whole. Making offerings to deities might not seem like it can help you get to know yourself better, but offerings allow you to strengthen your bond between them and your deities, and this helps them have an energetic anchor within your life. Making offerings to deities or even just your spiritual guide is a wonderful way to symbolize respect, gratitude, and dedication, as well as heighten your bond.

Offerings help you get to know your deities as well as yourself because they give you the chance to learn about them as well as yourself. In specific, you are able to learn more about your aspirations, goals, dreams, and spiritual path through providing these offerings. What you hope for in return says a lot about you, and what you consider offering up does as well.

Devotion

Devotion keeps you pure of heart and in alignment with Ma'at, and is another way that you can cultivate a relationship with yourself. As you devote yourself to the Netjeru, your practice, or even yourself, you remain in alignment with balance and the truth. You remind yourself of what is important to you as well as the specific principles of Ma'at, inviting oneness and interconnectedness into your life. Through this deep connection with the divine that you can seek from devotion, you are able to learn more about yourself too. As you devote yourself, you learn more about your values and strengths, as well as areas in which you feel your spiritual practice is lacking. This, in turn, allows you to connect with yourself and your spirituality more in-depth

Spiritual Healing

Next on the list of ways that you can cultivate a strong relationship with yourself is spiritual healing, which encompasses various practices aimed at promoting well-being, balance, and harmony on a spiritual level. Some common methods of spiritual healing include energy healing such as Reiki and Pranic healing, Past life regression, Transpersonal therapy, Sound healing, Art therapy, Bodywork, Breathwork, and Yoga. Engaging in practices like these can help you release energetic and emotional blockages, which can promote and encourage healing on a deeper level. Oftentimes, it is really easy for us to wonder why we feel so stagnant in life, only for that stagnation to be due to some blockage that we had not noticed. Taking the time to clear up these blockages is a good way to tune into what you feel and think with some more depth.

Additionally, these practices are considered to be a form of self-care, and self-care is crucial. Self-care allows you to nurture your physical, emotional, and spiritual well-being, which helps you maintain a positive relationship with yourself. People who care about themselves enough to engage in these practices are more likely to experience heightened emotional connection, decreased stress, and other benefits as well.

Grounding

Often when we begin working in the spiritual realms, we may experience light body symptoms due to the higher vibrational energies we are working with. Grounding can be a way to help alleviate these symptoms as well as a way to connect deeper to yourself. To stay grounded and alleviate light body symptoms caused by an influx of spiritual information, engage in grounding practices. These may include standing barefoot in saltwater or on other natural surfaces like grass, soil or sand to connect with the Earth's energy. Another effective method involves sitting against a tree, nourishing both body and spirit with food and drink. Additionally, visualizing tree roots extending from your root chakra, situated at the base of the spine near the coccyx, deep into the core of the Earth, can foster connection and stability. When experiencing these symptoms, it is important to temporarily ease off from intense spiritual activities and give yourself time to integrate and consolidate the knowledge and experiences you have gained. This adjustment is part of an energetic process.

I will also point out here that light body symptoms are as vast as they are subjective and can be experienced as physical, emotional, and/or spiritual sensations. It is essential to approach any symptoms with an open mind and seek professional medical advice if you are unsure about their cause or if they are causing significant distress. While these symptoms can be associated with spiritual growth, they can also have physical or psychological origins.

Remember that cultivating a relationship with yourself is an ongoing journey that requires dedication, patience, and compassion. There is no need to rush this journey, it's not a race but a lifelong process of self-discovery and transformation.

Magic and Manifestation

I want to round off this chapter with a discussion of magic and manifestation. The word Heka is representative of the ancient Egyptian concept of magic. In Kemetic spirituality, Heka holds great significance. It is another important concept that you will need to be at least somewhat familiar with due to its importance to Kemetic spirituality. Heka represents the vital life force and power of creative energy that permeates the universe. In its essence, Heka is the cosmic energy running between all of us, connecting all beings and ideas to one another. In the context of Kemetic spirituality, Heka is not seen as a supernatural force; rather, it is seen as a natural force that individuals can harness and direct. In other words, Heka is not considered to be something mystical but instead something we can freely direct ourselves.

Respect and Reverence in Magic

Magic was considered a sacred art in ancient Egypt, which reflects in some of the beliefs regarding Kemetic spirituality today, especially in reconstructionist circles. Those who practiced magic in ancient Egypt did so with a very deep respect and reverence for both the divine and the natural world. This means that one was not treated as more special than the other; both the natural world and the magical one were considered and valued as one and the same. Practitioners of magic understood that their intentions and actions alike could have very profound impacts on the world around them. As a result, those who practiced magic approached it with a sense of responsibility and ethical considerations, both of which shine through in the principles of Ma'at that practitioners still abide by today.

Thoughts, Words, Emotions, and Actions as Potent Magic

Another facet of Kemetic spirituality to understand is that Kemetic spirituality treats and recognizes the fact that thoughts, words, emotions, and actions are all expressions of Heka. This means that there was a resounding acknowledgment that these concepts had the ability to shape reality. Moreover, it was recognized that individuals could generate energies that have the ability to be either positive or negative. These energies can also make an impact, influencing the outcomes of their creator's life as well as the world around them. As a result of this fact, it is important for those who wish to practice Heka to be mindful of their inner states as well as their external expressions. Doing so will prevent unintended consequences, as well as help a practitioner become stronger at manifesting their desired outcome. One easy way to do this is to practice daily affirmations to align yourself with positive energies and manifest your desires.

Harnessing the Power of Intention

Intention is a major factor involved in Heka, magic, and manifestation. The intention is just what it sounds like—the intent you have for a magical working. In other words, intention can be the goal that you set or the outcome that you expect to arise from a magical endeavor. Intention can be on purpose or subconscious, but the best intentions work when they are clear and focused. Clear and focused intentions allow people like you and me to align ourselves with the flow of Heka and then direct that intention toward our goals. One of the primary skills involved in utilizing intention is visualizing and feeling the desired outcome—usually, as if your intention has already been achieved. This helps one to foster a strong sense of belief in their manifestation as well as their desires.

Learning from Positive and Negative Experiences

Learning from positive and negative experiences is not just a part of truth and knowledge seeking—it also plays a role in Heka and manifestation too. When one practices magic and manifestation, a good practitioner is one who embraces the lessons they learn from positive experiences as well as negative ones—because everything we encounter, good or bad, has something valuable to teach us. A good practitioner understands that setbacks and challenges, for example, can offer valuable insights that allow us to grow both as people and as spiritual beings. By reflecting on experiences of all varieties, practitioners can refine their intentions and approaches to magic as a result of these reflections, thus strengthening their ability to manifest what they wish to manifest more effectively.

The Interplay of Magic and Free Will

The interplay of magic and free will is another important concept to understand. In Kemetic spirituality, the connection that exists between free will and magic is widely respected. Practitioners are aware of the fact that magic can influence outcomes, including other individuals. However, they are also aware of the fact that the choices and actions of others can influence those very same outcomes. In other words, those who practice magic know that their choices can impact a situation just like the free will of others involved can. Because of this, it is common for a practitioner to hope to use magic in order to harmonize their intention within the broader flow of life while simultaneously respecting the agency of all beings. There are certain avenues of magic that do involve the violation of the agency of others, but those are not what Kemetic spirituality typically entails.

Personal Transformation through Magic

Magic is also beneficial outside of the realm of manifesting external desires. Outside of just manifesting their desires, Kemetic practitioners understand that magic can be an aid for personal growth and transformation as well. Heka and working with it can empower practitioners to identify and release limiting beliefs, fears, negative thought patterns, and more. This allows for profound inner shifts to occur, which facilitates a deeper connection with one's higher self. And, of course, we cannot forget harmony with Ma'at.

Overall, magic and manifestation serve as integral parts of Kemetic spirituality, both of which are grounded in the profound understanding of Heka as the creative life force. By nurturing relationships with the Netjeru, understanding oneself, and tapping into the energy of magic, Kemetic practitioners embark on a transformative path that brings growth, evolution, expanded consciousness, and an overall better life.

Chapter Five

Connecting with the Kemetic Pantheon

"The body is the house of God. Man, know thyself...and thou shalt know the Gods." —Ancient Egyptian Proverb

In the ancient land of Egypt, spirituality was intricately intertwined with the worship and veneration of a vast and diverse pantheon of gods and goddesses. These deities were not merely distant figures in myths and legends; they were living forces deeply ingrained in the hearts and minds of the ancient Egyptians. To connect with the pantheon of ancient Egyptian deities is to embark on a profound and transformative journey in Kemetic spirituality.

This chapter delves into the mystical realm of ancient Egyptian gods and goddesses, exploring their significance and providing valuable guidance on how to establish and nurture meaningful relationships with them. The belief in divine beings, each with unique attributes and powers, formed the foundation of

Kemetic spirituality, offering devotees an opportunity to seek guidance, protection, and blessings from the celestial realm.

Figure 1: Egyptian Deities

Importance of Living with the Netjeru: An Exploration of Divine Connection

Living with the Netjeru, the ancient Egyptian deities, holds immense significance in Kemetic spirituality. The exchange of sacred energy between humans and the gods forms a powerful dynamic that fuels spiritual growth, wisdom, and transformative experiences. The Netjeru, in turn, prioritizes human evolution and remains closely connected to the planet and its inhabitants, creating a profound and enduring relationship that propels life forward on both the individual and cosmic levels.

Exchange of Sacred Energy: Nourishing Spiritual Growth

Within the scope of Kemetic spirituality, there is a divine connection with the Netjeru, which involves a constant flow of energy between the human realm on Earth and the immortal realm of the gods. This exchange is not one that is one-sided; rather, it is a dynamic interaction that nurtures spiritual growth and enlightenment while benefiting both sides of the dynamic evenly. It is one of mutual benefit, in other words, which means that there is no party at a disadvantage from participating in the exchange. Instead, both parties have everything to gain. It is when individuals open both their minds and hearts to the divine forces that they invite the presence of gods and goddesses alike into their life. This is what creates a sacred bond with the ability to transcend time and space.

There are many different ways in which a relationship between humans and the Netjeru is kindled. Through rituals, prayers, offerings, and acts of devotion, individuals offer their love, gratitude, and reverence to the Netjeru. In return, the deities bless their devotees with divine guidance, protection, and wisdom. This is a mutually symbiotic relationship with the ability to nurture and nourish the soul, enriching it with profound experiences, revelations, and transformative insights. This relationship further serves as a consistent reminder that the presence of the divine is always available—which is in alignment with the Kemetic ideal that the divine and the human world are connected—offering supportive and guiding advice to those in all stages of a spiritual journey.

Propelling Life Forward: Embracing Cosmic Purpose

A perception that the Netjeru are distant or aloof beings is one that is very misguided; the Netjeru are active participants in a beautiful cosmic dance that represents life, influencing the Earth and those who reside upon it every single day. Intricately woven into the fabric of creation, the presence of the Netjeru serves to guide the forces of nature, cycles of life, and the destinies of humanity. By living in harmony with the Netjeru, individuals align themselves with the larger cosmic purpose, understanding that they are part of a grand, interconnected web of existence.

One of the top priorities of the Netjeru is human evolution—they want to see us grow and succeed, doing well in everything that we do. As a result, the Netjeru nurture and safeguard the growth and development of those of us on Earth. Offering inspiration, courage, and strength are just a few of the things that the Netjeru offers to us, guiding us through the trials and tribulations of life while also celebrating moments of joy where available. This cosmic partnership infuses individuals with a sense of purpose and direction, knowing that they are co-creators in the grand tapestry of life.

Closeness to the Planet: Guardians of Earth and Its Inhabitants

In other belief systems, deities are perceived to be distant beings that are separate, better than, or simply more than human beings in some manner. But unlike these distant deities of other belief systems, the Netjeru—every single deity that comprises it—remains closely connected to Earth and all of us who inhabit it. According to ancient Egyptian cosmic principles, the gods and goddesses were never confined to some distant celestial realm or heavens. No, they were prevalent and free to roam the natural world. This immanence allowed them to act as guardians and protectors, nurturing the well-being of the land, its people, and its creatures.

By recognizing the divine presence within the earthly realm, individuals in Kemetic spirituality develop a profound sense of interconnectedness with the environment. This awareness then fosters something of a deep sense of respect and responsibility—alongside love and fondness—for the Earth and its resources. Kemeticism urges its practitioners to act as stewards of the plant. Living in harmony with the Netjeru includes caring for the environment, respecting all living beings, and preserving the natural world for future generations, all of which you learn to do by remaining in alignment with Ma'at and continuously moving forward in your spiritual journey.

Empowerment and Guidance on Life's Journey

As a whole, the Kemetic pantheon offers a spring of empowerment and guidance to those who seek wisdom and counsel from them. Each deity embodies distinct attributes and qualities, which we will talk about in-depth soon. However, to give a few examples:

- The wisdom of Thoth, the god of knowledge and writing, aids in scholarly pursuits and intellectual growth.

- The nurturing and protective qualities of Hathor offer solace and comfort during challenging times.

- The strength and determination of Sekhmet empower individuals to face adversity with courage.

- The guidance of Ma'at, the goddess of truth and justice, helps individuals navigate ethical dilemmas and maintain balance in their lives.

By forming such a deep connection with specific deities that resonate with your individual needs, you can empower yourself to find plentiful support, love, and guidance from the Netjeru—they act as compassionate mentors, assisting individuals in finding their true path, embracing their unique gifts, and fulfilling their life's purpose.

Living among the Netjeru is a profound, transformative experience that has the capacity to unite us human beings with the spiritual realm. There is an exchange of sacred energy between us humans and the gods we live among, which promotes spiritual growth, wisdom, purpose, and divine support within the mix of life. Safeguarding us humans, the Netjeru prioritizes us and our success, which is quite lovely if you ask me. This cosmic partnership propels life forward, encouraging individuals like you and me to embrace their unique role in the grand idea that is existence.

By recognizing the imminence of the Netjeru within the natural world, individuals become guardians of the planet, fostering a sense of interconnectedness and responsibility for the Earth and all its inhabitants. The divine guidance and empowerment bestowed by the Netjeru enriches the spiritual journey, offering insights, solace, and strength during life's trials and triumphs.

In all, living among the Netjeru is a harmonious dance of divine connection—a partnership that is sacred and elevates us through reverence, devotion, and open-mindedness. With this, we can walk hand in loving hands with the Netjeru, finding profound transformation and spiritual fulfillment along the way.

Key Deities in Kemetic Spirituality

Being as massive and timeless as it is, the Kemetic pantheon of deities comprises a rich and diverse selection of gods and goddesses, with some estimates suggesting there could be several hundred divine beings. Each deity within this pantheon embodies unique characteristics, powers, and symbolism, contributing to the intricate tapestry of Kemetic spirituality. These deities are not just figures of worship; they hold profound significance in shaping the beliefs, rituals, and the overall worldview of the ancient Egyptians.

The Netjeru, or gods and goddesses, are central to Kemetic spirituality, and their presence is felt in every aspect of the ancient Egyptian understanding of the cosmos. Key deities play pivotal roles within the cosmic order, representing fundamental principles such as creation, transformation, and balance. For example, Ra, the sun god, symbolizes the life-giving force of the sun, while Osiris represents the cycle of life, death, and rebirth. The ancient Egyptians believed that by aligning themselves with these deities and understanding their attributes, they could harmonize with the natural order and navigate the complexities of life and the afterlife.

As practitioners embark on their journey into Kemetic spirituality, exploring the idiosyncratic and fantastic aspects of essential deities becomes a gateway to understanding the intricate interplay of forces that governed the Egyptian worldview. Each deity is a living embodiment of cosmic principles, and delving into their myths and symbolism provides insights into the profound spiritual teachings that guided the ancient Egyptians in their quest for balance, wisdom, and connection with the divine.

Please note that we will be employing the contemporary names for the deities in the pages below and throughout this book, the original Kemetic names will be provided in parentheses. These modern names are crafted by contemporary practitioners, scholars, or enthusiasts in an effort to present the ancient Egyptian deities in a manner that is both accessible and pronounceable in today's languages.

Anubis (Anpu)

Anubis, the enigmatic jackal-headed god, stands as a guardian and guide of the deceased in the afterlife. As the god of embalming and funerary rites, Anubis played a crucial role in the mummification process and the preparation of the deceased for their journey to the afterlife. His iconic jackal head symbolizes his association with death and his ability to navigate the liminal space between life and the afterlife.

Anubis was believed to protect the souls of the deceased during their journey to the hall of judgment and ensure they received fair treatment in the afterlife. His role as a psychopomp, guiding souls through the perilous underworld, underscores the ancient Egyptians' deep belief in the existence of an afterlife and the importance of proper burial and funerary rituals. In art and mythology, Anubis is often depicted with a scale, representing the weighing of the heart against the feather of Ma'at. His presence at the judgment hall reinforced the idea that judgment in the afterlife was an impartial process based on one's actions and adherence to ethical principles during their lifetime.

Anubis's influence extended beyond the realm of death; he was also seen as a deity who offered solace to grieving families. The rituals performed under his guidance were not only a means to ensure a smooth transition to the afterlife but also a source of comfort for those left behind. In honoring Anubis, the ancient Egyptians found reassurance in the belief that their departed loved ones were under the watchful care of a compassionate and knowledgeable guide on their journey to the next life.

Bastet (Bast)

Bastet, was initially depicted as the benevolent and fierce lioness-headed goddess, however her image evolved over time to incorporate more gentle and domestic attributes. Bastet became closely linked with the domestic cat and eventually became one of the most popular and beloved deities in ancient Egypt. Bastet commands reverence as the patroness of home, fertility, protection, and joy. Her name derives from the ancient Egyptian word "bast," meaning "devourer," which reflects her fierce and protective aspects. Bastet was associated with the domestic sphere, safeguarding households and families from malevolent forces and harmful influences.

As a goddess of fertility and joy, Bastet brought merriment and celebration to the lives of the ancient Egyptians. Festivals in her honor were vibrant and lively, featuring music, dancing, and revelry. Her nurturing nature extended to her role as a protective deity, ensuring the safety and well-being of her devotees. In depictions, Bastet was often portrayed with a lioness or domestic cat head, the latter representing her more playful and gentle attributes. The domestic cat, revered for its protective and affectionate nature, became a sacred animal associated with Bastet. Cats were cherished and revered in ancient Egyptian society, and harming a cat, even accidentally, was a serious offense punishable by law.

Bastet's widespread popularity and influence endured for centuries, making her a symbol of both strength and nurturing care in the ancient Egyptian pantheon. Her legacy continues in the modern world, where she remains an iconic representation of feline grace, protection, and the harmonious balance between power and gentleness.

Hathor (Ḥwt-Ḥr)

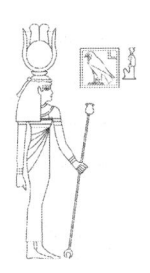

Hathor embodies a multifaceted divine presence associated with joy, music, dance, love, and motherhood. Her name, "Ḥwt-Ḥr," translates to "House of Horus," emphasizing her role as a nurturing and protective goddess. Hathor is often depicted with the head of a cow, adorned with a sun disc and cow horns, symbolizing her connection to both lunar and solar elements. This divine imagery signifies her dual nature, embracing the gentleness of a nurturing mother and the power of a celestial goddess.

As the personification of joy and celebration, Hathor played a crucial role in Egyptian religious festivals and rituals. She was invoked during times of festivities, music, and dance, fostering an atmosphere of communal jubilation. Her benevolent influence extended to aspects of love and fertility, with many seeking her guidance for matters related to romance, conception, and childbirth. Hathor was also revered as a protective deity, safeguarding individuals on their life journeys and in the afterlife.

In addition to her nurturing aspects, Hathor had connections to the divine cosmic order, representing the feminine counterpart to the sun god Ra. She was sometimes identified with the goddess Sekhmet, a more formidable aspect associated with the destructive power of the sun. This duality showcased the varied facets of Hathor's personality, from the gentle and nurturing mother to the powerful and protective goddess. Temples dedicated to Hathor, such as the famous complex at Dendera, served as centers of worship and celebration, emphasizing the enduring significance of this revered deity in ancient Egyptian culture.

Horus (Ḥr)

Horus is best known as a symbol of kingship, protection, and celestial power. The Egyptian name for Horus, "Ḥr" or "Heru," underscores his association with the falcon, a bird considered sacred and powerful in ancient Egyptian culture. As a falcon-headed god, Horus embodies the divine connection between the earthly and celestial realms, with his vigilant and watchful presence symbolizing the sky and its cosmic order.

One of the most prominent myths featuring Horus is the Osiris myth, where he avenges the murder of his father Osiris by his uncle Seth. The conflict between Horus and Seth represents the eternal struggle between order and chaos, and Horus emerges triumphant, securing his place as the rightful heir and symbol of legitimate kingship. As such, many pharaohs identified with Horus during their reign, believing that they were the earthly manifestation of this powerful deity, ensuring the continuity of Ma'at—the ancient Egyptian concept of cosmic balance and justice.

Horus' protective and watchful nature extends to his role as the patron deity of the pharaohs and the embodiment of the living king. The Eye of Horus, a symbol often associated with protection and healing, represents the falcon's eye and is a popular and enduring symbol in ancient Egyptian iconography. Temples dedicated to Horus, such as the grand Temple of Horus at Edfu, were constructed to honor and venerate this significant deity, emphasizing his enduring importance in the religious and cultural landscape of ancient Egypt.

Isis (Aset)

Among the revered goddesses of the Egyptian pantheon, Isis holds a prominent place as a paragon of magic, motherhood, healing, and protection. Her name translates to "throne" or "seat," symbolizing her role as the divine queen and protector of the throne of Egypt. Isis is renowned for her unwavering love and devotion, as she played a central role in the resurrection of her husband, Osiris, after his tragic demise at the hands of Set.

Her role as a nurturing mother goddess is a defining aspect of her persona, as she provided solace and compassion to her devotees, embracing them in her loving embrace during times of need. As a powerful healer and magician, Isis is often invoked in rituals and spells aimed at seeking guidance, protection, and divine intervention. Her influence extended beyond the earthly realm, as she was considered a benevolent goddess of the afterlife, offering her guidance and support to the souls on their journey to the judgment hall of Osiris.

Over time, the worship of Isis spread beyond Egypt, and what is known as the "cult of Isis" gained popularity throughout the Mediterranean region, particularly during the Hellenistic and Roman periods. The decline of the cult of Isis occurred with the rise of Christianity, which led to the suppression of traditional pagan practices. The last known temples dedicated to Isis were closed in the 6th century CE.

Ma'at (Ma'at)

Ma'at is more than just a concept—she is a goddess as well. Central to the ethical and spiritual framework of ancient Egyptian society was the concept of Ma'at. Ma'at is both a goddess and a concept, representing truth, justice, balance, and harmony in the universe. She personifies the cosmic order and the moral principles that govern existence, ensuring cosmic harmony and stability. Ma'at is often depicted with an ostrich feather on her head, symbolizing truth and balance.

In the afterlife judgment, the heart of the deceased is weighed against Ma'at's feather to determine if the individual lived a virtuous and righteous life. If the heart was found lighter than the feather, it signified a life in harmony with Ma'at's principles, ensuring the soul's safe passage to the afterlife. This concept permeated all aspects of Egyptian life, from governance and law to personal ethics and social behavior.

The devotion to Ma'at highlights the ancient Egyptians' belief in the importance of living a just and balanced life, promoting a society in which truth, fairness, and compassion were revered virtues. By upholding the principles of Ma'at, individuals ensured cosmic order and contributed to the well-being and prosperity of their communities.

Osiris (Asar)

Osiris, one of the central deities in ancient Egyptian mythology, holds sway as the god of the afterlife, rebirth, and fertility. As the brother and husband of Isis and the father of Horus, Osiris represents the cycle of life, death, and regeneration. He serves as the divine judge in the afterlife, presiding over the judgment of souls in the hall of Ma'at, where the hearts of the deceased are weighed against her feather.

Osiris's role in Egyptian spirituality showcases the belief in the continuity of life beyond death, as he guides the souls of the righteous to eternal life in the Fields of Yaru, the idyllic paradise of the afterlife. He embodies the transformative power of death, teaching the ancient Egyptians that life is a continuous journey of growth and spiritual evolution. Osiris's annual death and rebirth, symbolized by the Nile's annual flooding, were significant events in the Egyptian calendar and served as a reminder of the cyclical nature of existence.

Osiris's influence extends beyond the realms of death and judgment, as he embodies the agricultural cycle and fertility. Associated with the annual flooding of the Nile, Osiris symbolizes the renewal of life and the prosperity brought by the inundation. His myth further emphasizes the interconnectedness of the natural world and spiritual beliefs in ancient Egypt, portraying Osiris not only as a judge of the afterlife but also as a vital force in the perpetual rejuvenation of the land. This dual role underscores the depth of Osiris's significance in Egyptian cosmology, representing both the cosmic order and the life-sustaining forces integral to the civilization's agricultural success.

Ra (Re)

Ra, revered as the Sun God of light, warmth, and creation, stands at the pinnacle of the Egyptian pantheon as a radiant god, serving as the physical manifestation of the sun. Often depicted with a falcon head crowned with a solar disc, symbolizing the sun, Ra is accompanied by the sacred cobra, Uraeus, as a protective symbol. Representing the eternal cycle of both light and darkness, as well as warmth and illumination, Ra embodies the primordial force of creation, sustaining all living beings with life-giving energy.

As Ra journeys across the sky from sunrise to sunset, his symbolic passage represents the cyclical nature of existence and the passage of time. At sunset, Ra begins his nightly journey through the underworld, facing challenges and threats that symbolize the nocturnal aspects of the sun and its subsequent rebirth at dawn. Each dawn marks Ra's daily rebirth, exemplifying the theme of eternal renewal and emphasizing the belief in the cyclical nature of life, death, and rebirth. According to myth, Ra's tears are said to have created humanity, illustrating the profound interconnectedness between Ra and the created world.

The ancient Egyptians held Ra in the highest esteem, regarding him as the divine ruler, the king of gods, and the ultimate source of all life. Temples dedicated to Ra were meticulously aligned to capture the initial rays of the sun during special occasions, symbolizing the sacred connection between Ra and humanity. Constructed with precise alignment, these temples emphasized the divine connection that exists between Ra and humanity.

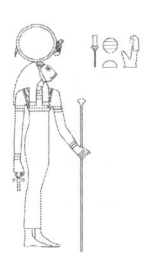

Sekhmet (Sḫmt)

Sekhmet, a formidable and revered goddess in ancient Egyptian mythology, embodies the dual nature of ferocity and healing. The Egyptian name for Sekhmet, written as "Sḫmt," reflects her association with power and might. Often depicted as a lioness-headed deity or as a woman with the head of a lioness, Sekhmet is the embodiment of divine wrath and protection. As the daughter of Ra, the sun god, Sekhmet is intimately connected with solar power, symbolizing the scorching heat of the sun and the fierce aspect of cosmic order.

One of the prominent myths involving Sekhmet centers around her role as a warrior unleashed by Ra to punish humanity for its disobedience. In the tale, Sekhmet's rage becomes uncontrollable, leading to the potential destruction of all life. To mitigate the devastation, Ra tricks Sekhmet into consuming a large quantity of red beer, which she mistakes for blood, causing her to become intoxicated and pacified. This story highlights Sekhmet's dual nature as both a fierce and destructive force and a deity capable of being appeased and transformed for the greater good.

Despite her wrathful aspect, Sekhmet is also associated with healing and protection. In her gentler form, she is sometimes called upon for assistance in matters of health and well-being. Temples dedicated to Sekhmet, such as the one at Karnak, were places of worship and healing rituals, attesting to the belief in her ability to both inflict and alleviate suffering. Sekhmet remains a captivating figure in ancient Egyptian mythology, embodying the intricate balance between destruction and restoration, power and compassion.

Thoth (Djehuty)

Last but certainly not least, we encounter Thoth, the ibis-headed god, occupying a vital role in the Egyptian pantheon as the divine scribe, keeper of wisdom, and master of magical knowledge. Credited as the inventor of hieroglyphs, the sacred script used for religious texts and monumental inscriptions, Thoth's name is derived from the Egyptian word 'Djehuty,' meaning 'he who is like the ibis,' symbolizing the sacred bird that represents wisdom and knowledge.

In his capacity as the divine scribe, Thoth recorded the deeds and events of both gods and humanity. He served as the mediator and arbitrator of disputes among the gods, embodying wisdom, logic, and intellect in all his endeavors. Thoth's association with writing and language elevated him to the role of the patron of scholars and seekers of knowledge; ancient Egyptian scribes universally worshipped him, with many adorning their 'offices' with paintings of Thoth.

Depicted in ancient Egyptian art with an ibis head or as a baboon, symbolizing his connection with wisdom and lunar cycles, Thoth played a vital role as the god of magic and science. His influence extended beyond the realms of intellect and wisdom, making him a multifaceted deity revered for his contributions to language, magic, and the pursuit of enlightenment. Thoth's essential role in healing rituals and magical practices further solidified his position, bestowing blessings upon those who sought his guidance.

The key deities in Kemetic spirituality represent profound cosmic archetypes, embodying the fundamental forces that govern life, death, and spiritual transformation. Anubis, Bastet, Hathor, Horus, Isis, Ma'at, Osiris, Ra, Sekhmet, and Thoth are not merely distant entities in myths; they are living forces that guide, protect, and inspire their devotees. The worship of these deities was at the heart of the ancient Egyptians' spiritual life, shaping their beliefs, ethics, and cultural practices.

By exploring and understanding these divine personalities, individuals can tap into the timeless wisdom and eternal truths that have resonated throughout human history. Their stories and attributes continue to inspire seekers of wisdom and spiritual enlightenment, reminding humanity of the profound interconnectedness between the mortal and the divine realms. The legacy of these key deities endures, as their ancient wisdom offers valuable insights and guidance to modern spiritual seekers on their journey of self-discovery and cosmic understanding.

Connecting With the Pantheon

In Kemetic spirituality, connecting with the pantheon of ancient Egyptian deities is a transformative and profound experience that nurtures the soul and enriches one's spiritual journey. Each deity embodies unique qualities and energies, resonating with individuals in different ways. Let's discuss, specifically, some of the ways that you can connect with the Kemetic pantheon.

Follow Your Intuition to Identify Resonant Deities

One of the best ways to embark upon a strong connection with this pantheon is to learn to trust your intuition in order to identify particularly resonant deities who you may wish to work with. Allow your intuition and inner guidance to lead you toward picking a deity that resonates with you personally. In order to help the process, make sure to read about various gods and goddesses within the Egyptian pantheon—as I only gave you a small taste of all the deities that there are to work with. Explore the ancient myths surrounding these deities, and pay attention to ones that evoke a particular sense of warmth or familiarity within you. Using your intuition as a compass, you will be guided toward the proper divine energies for your unique spiritual needs.

Engage in Acts of Devotion and Create Offerings

Devotion is the most prominent way that you can show your deities that you love and appreciate them. Through acts of reverence as well as offerings, you can display very sincere love and gratitude toward the members of the pantheon that you work with—or even the pantheon as a whole. Craft or present offerings that are meaningful to the specific deities you plan to honor, including food, drinks, incense, flowers, or symbolic objects that align with that particular deity. These offerings symbolize your willingness to give and receive, establishing a sacred exchange of energy between you and the divine.

Create a Dedicated Altar or Sacred Space

We talked about it earlier, but truly, setting aside a sacred space is a wonderful way to honor your deities. Designate a sacred space or altar within your home where you can focus your spiritual practices and connect with the divine. Decorate this space with symbols, images, and offerings that represent the deities you seek to commune with. This sacred altar becomes a focal point for your

AWAKENING THE SACRED FLAME: A BEGINNER'S GUIDE...

spiritual journey, a portal where you can open your heart and mind to the divine presence.

Practice Invocations to Call Upon Divine Presences

An invocation is a ritualistic or spoken prayer that calls upon the presence, guidance, and blessings of the divine. It is a sacred invitation, a way to establish a tangible connection with the spiritual realm and invite the specific deities to be present and actively involved in your sacred space or life. During an invocation, use heartfelt words, expressing your reverence and desire to connect with the divine energies. Share your intentions and seek guidance, protection, and blessings from the gods and goddesses you are invoking.

One example of an invocation that you may use in your practice is as follows:

"Divine [Name of Deity or Divine Essence], I call upon your presence and grace.

In this sacred moment, I open my heart and mind to your divine energy.

May your wisdom and love flow through me, guiding my steps on this sacred path.

I seek your guidance, protection, and blessings, as I embark on this journey of [state the purpose or intention].

With reverence and humility, I welcome your presence, and I offer my sincere devotion and gratitude.

Thank you, thank you, thank you."

Practice Meditation and Visualization Techniques

Meditation and visualization are powerful techniques—ones I've mentioned throughout the course of the book. As it turns out, meditation and visualization alike can help you get to know and bond with your deities as well. Through meditation, you have the ability to quiet your mind and open yourself to receive various insights and guidance from the divine realm. Practices of visualization allow you to imagine yourself in the presence of your deities, fostering an immaculate sense of closeness and communion with the Netjeru. As you meditate and visualize, allow yourself to be receptive to any messages or images that may come forth from the divine. In my own meditation, I often visualize myself visiting the Temple of Isis.

Participate in Rituals and Celebrations

Participating in rituals and celebrations dedicated to specific deities or important dates in the Kemetic calendar creates a sense of community and unity with fellow spiritual seekers. These collective experiences not only deepen your connection with the divine but also amplify the energies of the rituals, making the experience even more potent and transformative. The ancient Egyptians celebrated numerous festivals, referred to as "heb," each holding significance too vast to comprehensively address here. The exact dates of these festivals hinged on precise astronomical observations and local variations within ancient Egypt. Consequently, pinpointing specific Gregorian calendar dates for these events proves challenging. Modern Kemetic reconstructionists and practitioners may choose to celebrate these festivals based on their own interpretations, sometimes aligning with astronomical events or using reconstructed Kemetic calendars. If you are interested in modern celebrations, you may find communities who follow Kemetic spirituality to discover more information on their practices and observances.

Study Ancient Egyptian Texts

Immerse yourself in the study of ancient Egyptian texts, such as the Pyramid Texts, the Coffin Texts, the Book of the Dead, The Wisdom Literature, The Instructions of Ankhsheshonq, and other hymns, and prayers dedicated to the gods and goddesses. These texts provide profound insights into the mythology, beliefs, and roles of the deities in ancient Egyptian society. Through the study of these sacred writings, you gain a deeper understanding of the divine energies and the wisdom that has been passed down through the ages. Included at the end of this book is an extensive list of additional reading materials for those who may be interested in further exploration.

Establish a Dialogue and Commune with the Deities

To truly establish a profound connection with the pantheon, cultivate a sincere and personal dialogue with the deities. Approach them with humility and an open heart, inviting them into your life as guides, protectors, and sources of inspiration. In this sacred communion, be open to receiving messages and guidance from the divine. These messages and guidance may come through one of your clair senses, or if these are not yet activated, they may emerge in dreams, thoughts, or present themselves as subtle signs in your daily life. In the beginning of my journey I used the Isis Oracle Deck and Auset Egyptian Oracle Cards[1] to assist me in receiving messages from the divine. You may also wish to keep a journal to record your thoughts, feelings, and any divine revelations that may come to you during your moments of communion.

In the next chapter, I'll take a closer look into the fascinating methods of establishing dialogue and communion with the Kemetic Pantheon through divination tools and practices, including a bonus chapter on dream interpretation.

***

Connecting with the pantheon of ancient Egyptian deities is an awe-inspiring journey of self-discovery and spiritual growth. By following your intuition, engaging in acts of devotion, creating a sacred space, practicing invocations, meditating, participating in rituals, studying ancient texts, and establishing a sincere dialogue, you open pathways to the divine energies that have endured throughout time. The gods and goddesses become your allies, guiding and illuminating your path in Kemetic spirituality. As you embrace the divine within and without, your connection with the pantheon becomes a profound reflection of the eternal dance between humanity and the sacred cosmos.

Approach Practicing With Sincerity and Respect

Within the mystical world of Kemetic spirituality, connecting to the pantheon is an intricate and transformative journey that is not restricted by time nor space. In order to embark on this profound path with divine communion, seekers of spiritual journeys must approach the path—as well as the Netjeru—with the utmost sincerity, respect, and an open mind and heart. The process of establishing meaningful relationships with the divine is multifaceted and requires a deep understanding of both the mortal and immortal realms. Let's delve into the intricacies of approaching the pantheon with authenticity, humility, and reverence, allowing for the profound communion to unfold.

At the core of connecting with the pantheon lies the essence of sincerity and authenticity. Seekers are encouraged to be true to themselves, embracing their unique selves and individual spiritual journeys. Embracing authenticity allows for a genuine connection with the divine, unfiltered by external expectations or societal norms. This authenticity creates a harmonious resonance between the mortal and immortal realms, nurturing a relationship based on truth and a genuine desire for communion.

The gods and goddesses of the pantheon are not mere mythological figures but cosmic archetypes representing the fundamental forces of the universe. As seekers approach them, it is crucial to acknowledge the sacredness and extensive wisdom they embody. Each deity holds a unique set of attributes, energies, and stories that provide valuable lessons and insights into human experience. Recognizing the divine as sacred cosmic beings helps seekers approach with a sense of awe and wonder, fostering a deeper connection.

Engaging with the pantheon requires humility and reverence, recognizing the inherent vastness and power of the gods and goddesses. Approaching them with a sense of humility reminds seekers of their place in the grand tapestry of existence and the interconnectedness of all life. This sense of reverence elevates communion from a simple interaction to a sacred exchange of energies, where seekers offer their devotion and seek guidance from the divine with the utmost respect.

Building relationships with these deities is not an overnight process. As seekers engage in rituals, prayers, and meditations to connect with the divine, they must remain patient and open to the unfolding of the relationship. Like a blossoming flower, each encounter and experience reveals new facets of the deities, deepening the bond over time. The natural progression of the relationship allows for a profound and authentic connection to flourish.

Consistency is essential in establishing and nurturing relationships with the divine. Regular communion through rituals, meditation, and prayer creates a sacred space for seekers to open their hearts and invite the presence of the gods and goddesses. As seekers engage in regular communion, they align their energies with the divine frequencies, creating a harmonious resonance that fosters a deeper connection and understanding.

The gods and goddesses are beacons of wisdom, and approaching them with sincerity and an open heart invites their guidance and insights into the seeker's life. Seeking guidance is not solely about seeking answers to specific questions; it is a powerful act of surrendering to the divine will and allowing the gods and goddesses to show the way. Through this act of surrender, seekers open themselves to receive profound revelations and transformative insights from the divine realm.

Devotion is a powerful and transformative force that strengthens the connection between mortal and divine. Expressing love, devotion, and gratitude through offerings, prayers, and acts of service is a way to honor the gods and goddesses and show appreciation for their presence and guidance. Offerings can be as simple as fresh water, food, incense, or handcrafted symbols of devotion. The act of giving with sincerity and love elevates the relationship to a sacred level of reciprocity.

As seekers approach the pantheon, it is crucial to maintain an open heart and an open mind. Release any preconceived notions or expectations, and approach the gods and goddesses with curiosity and a willingness to learn. The divine energies often work in mysterious ways, and remaining open allows seekers to be receptive to the subtle nuances of each encounter, unveiling the deeper truths within the connection.

In divine connection, sincerity, respect, and an open heart are the guiding steps that lead seekers closer to the gods and goddesses of the pantheon. As seekers embark on this transformative journey, they are invited to embrace their authenticity, offer reverence, and allow the relationships to unfold naturally. Within this profound communion, seekers discover the interconnectedness of all things as the divine energies inspire and guide them on their unique spiritual paths. The gods and goddesses welcome seekers with open arms and loving grace, inviting them into the mystical realm of cosmic communion, where the mortal and divine intertwine in a sacred dance of profound revelation and transformative growth.

Connecting with the pantheon of ancient Egyptian deities enriches one's spiritual journey in Kemetic spirituality. By fostering relationships with specific deities, practicing devotion, and engaging in rituals and study, practitioners can deepen their connection and receive the wisdom and blessings of the Netjeru.

---

1. You can find these cards on Amazon at the following links: Isis Oracle Deck: https://amzn.to/3s94yuG, Auset Egyptian Oracle Cards: https://amzn.to/3OzKjOd. As an Amazon Associate I earn from qualifying purchases.

Chapter Six

Navigating the Path with Divination Tools

"The divine speaks through the ordinary." —Malidoma Patrice Somé

In the last chapter, we discussed how to connect with the Kemetic Pantheon. In this chapter, we will discuss some specific ways in which you can do that through the use of divination tools.

Kemetic spirituality uses divination as a tool to connect with the divine, to garner wisdom and insights that might otherwise stay hidden. For the beginner, divination can feel often feel like trying to tune into a faint radio station, straining your ears to catch the elusive notes of your favorite song. But with time and practice, that song will gradually become clearer and clearer.

Now, let's delve into this fascinating topic. Divination in Kemetic Spirituality plays a critical role in three distinct ways.

First, it serves as a bridge between the human and the divine. For example, practitioners might use divination tools such as oracle cards or the casting of lots to receive messages from their deities. This isn't just hocus pocus; it's a deeply ingrained practice that links back to ancient times when priests and priestesses would use similar methods to talk with the gods.

Secondly, divination acts as a form of guidance in daily life. It's not about predicting the future, but about gaining insights into current situations. You might be facing a challenging decision and turn to divination for clarity. It's akin to asking for directions on a journey—you're still the one driving, but divination can help point out potential roadblocks or shortcuts.

Lastly, divination fosters personal growth and self-awareness. When you engage with divination, you're not just passively receiving messages. You're actively interpreting them, which can lead to a deeper understanding of yourself and your place in the world. It's like holding up a mirror to your soul—the reflections can be enlightening and sometimes even startling.

Divination in Kemetic Spirituality isn't about seeking easy answers or quick fixes. It's about forging a deeper connection with the divine and learning to navigate life's complexities with wisdom and grace.

There have been several studies linking spiritual practices like divination with improved mental health, such as reduced stress levels. Researchers at Duke University found that religious practices provide coping mechanisms during stressful times (Pargament et al., 2000). The act of engaging with divine entities through these tools can be therapeutic by providing comfort and guidance when needed most.

Dr. Auset Baskauskas's study on "The Spiritual Lives of Women" provides insight into how divination practices have empowered women by providing them with a sense of control over their lives (Baskauf, 2013). Her work showcases real-life examples of women finding clarity amidst chaos through these sacred tools.

Indeed, there have been many times throughout my own life where I have turned to divination tools to aid me in decision making, and to comfort me in times of personal crisis, as well as a means to connect with the divine.

So, the next time you're feeling lost or uncertain, remember this: divination isn't just a spiritual practice, it's a tool for life. It's like tuning into that elusive radio station—sometimes the signal might be faint, but with patience and practice, you can tune into the divine wisdom that's always there.

Analyzing your connection with the Kemetic Pantheon using divination tools requires introspection and awareness. It's about recognizing patterns, symbols, and messages that may appear abstract but carry profound meanings meant just for you. I have outlined some forms of divination below that you can consider, see what resonates most with you and go from there.

Intuition

Intuition, often referred to as inner wisdom or gut feeling, is not commonly thought of as a divination tool. Yet, it is indeed your most potent innate tool for this purpose. It is the subtle language of the soul that communicates through feelings, nudges, and insights beyond the realm of logical reasoning. When engaged consciously, intuition can guide you in making decisions, providing glimpses into the unseen and the unknown. In divination practices, tuning into your intuition involves quieting the mind, trusting the inner senses, and being receptive to subtle energies.

Whether faced with choices in daily life or seeking spiritual guidance, listening to your intuitive whispers can offer profound insights, helping you to navigate your life path with a deeper understanding of yourself and the universal forces at play. Recognizing intuition as a divination tool is acknowledging the interconnectedness between your conscious mind and the vast realms that exist beyond your immediate awareness.

In the early phases of cultivating your intuitive abilities, distinguishing and trusting your inner guidance may seem challenging amidst the constant noise of the mind. Here are some effective methods to cultivate your intuition during these initial stages:

- **Learn to distinguish between fear-based thoughts and true intuitive nudges.** Distinguishing between fear-based thoughts and authentic intuitive nudges involves honing a keen awareness of the subtle nuances in your internal landscape. Fear-based thoughts often manifest as anxious, repetitive, or catastrophic scenarios driven by worries about the future. In contrast, true intuitive nudges typically emerge spontaneously, carrying a sense of calm assurance and alignment with your core values.

- **Observe the emotional tone accompanying the thought.** Intuitive insights often bring a feeling of peace or resonance, while fear-based thoughts may evoke tension or discomfort. Additionally, consider the origin of the thought; intuitive nudges often arise from a deeper, quieter space within, while fear-based thoughts tend to be more reactive.

- **Take note of your initial impressions or gut instincts.** Intuition often communicates swiftly before the rational mind kicks in, so capturing these intuitive nudges in writing before the analytical mind takes over, provides a tangible record. Whether you decide to act on these intuitive nudges or not, by documenting them you can go back to them retrospectively to see if they were correct.

Regular mindfulness practices, such as meditation, can enhance your ability to discern these subtleties. With time and self-awareness, you can refine your capacity to distinguish between fear-driven mental chatter and the authentic guidance of your intuition. Discernment is nurtured through consistent practice and thoughtful reflection. Over time, these practices can enhance your ability to gauge the accuracy of your intuitive insights, fostering a deeper connection with your inner wisdom.

Oracle Cards

Oracle cards serve as an excellent and easy-to-use tool for divination—it's often been my go-to method. To start, find a deck that resonates with you. As I was working with goddess Isis (*Aset*) in the beginning of my journey, I used the Isis Oracle Deck and Auset Egyptian Oracle Cards[1]. Once you have chosen a deck, ensure you cleanse it, using sage or palo santo, and then spend some time to connect with each card before use.

Once you're ready to begin divination, carve out a sacred space and calm your mind through meditation or deep breathing exercises. Maintain a steady focus as you shuffle the deck, contemplating your question or topic of interest. When you sense it's time to stop shuffling, split the deck in half; place the bottom half over the top half, then choose the top card. This becomes your drawn card.

Alternatively, spread out the cards before you in an arc-like fan and choose several cards that resonate with you to form a meaningful arrangement. A commonly used arrangement includes three cards: one symbolizing the past, another reflecting your present situation, and the last pointing towards future possibilities. Oracle card decks often offer various spreads for you to explore too.

If any card jumps out of the deck whilst shuffling, as often happens—use your intuition to decide if this is 'the' card for your draw or if it should be set aside as extra information relevant to your query.

Each card will carry symbols and imagery that mirror aspects of divine realms or spiritual principles. They will also come with accompanying written interpretations. Let your intuition lead you when deciphering these cards; paying attention to the messages conveyed through the imagery, symbolism, and written interpretations. Contemplate how these cards connect with your question or circumstance while trusting in the Netjeru's wisdom for guidance and insight.

Through this process of communion with the divine, oracle cards can become a sacred tool for you to deepen your spiritual connection and navigate the complexities of life with clarity and purpose.

Casting Lots

Casting lots, an ancient form of divination, held a pivotal role in the spiritual practices of ancient Egypt. Priests and individuals alike often used this method to seek divine guidance. The procedure involved throwing objects—often marked stones, sticks or other small items—and interpreting the patterns or symbols they formed upon landing. Within religious rituals of ancient Egypt, casting lots served as a tool for decision-making, seeking advice on significant matters or deciphering the will of the gods. It was believed that the randomness inherent in casting allowed divine forces to sway the outcome, offering insights into future events or solutions to current issues. Skilled diviners who were adept at understanding symbolic language associated with these objects performed interpretation of these lots. Revered as a bridge to connect with spiritual realms, this practice provided access to divine wisdom on matters of great importance.

To initiate this practice for yourself, first choose your casting lots. Some examples are:

- Marked stones or pebbles with symbols or markings.

- Wooden pieces or tokens, each with distinct symbols or markings.

- Dice with markings or symbols.

- Metal tokens with engraved symbols.

- Seashells with specific markings or arrangements.

- Bone pieces with markings or engravings.

- Clay or wax figurines or shapes.

- Runes: Although originating from Germanic or Norse cultures and not traditionally used in Kemetic practices, modern-day practitioners have adopted them due to their easy availability and pre-existing markings suitable for divination—eliminating any need to create new ones.

Once you have chosen your lots, create a serene and consecrated space, acknowledging the presence of the gods and goddesses. Hold the lots in your hands and channel your spiritual energy into them. Focus your intention on a specific question or area of your life that seeks clarity. Cast them onto a consecrated surface, allowing the patterns and positions to form a unique configuration. Interpret the arrangement through your intuition, noting the symbols and their positions.

This ancient practice acts as an immediate connection to the divine; offering deep insights and guidance to those who approach it with reverence and openness. It's a reminder that, in the dance of the lots, the divine energies of Kemetic spirituality weave a tapestry of wisdom to illuminate your path.

Scrying

Scrying, an ancient divination practice, involves gazing into a reflective or translucent surface to uncover insights, visions, or answers. This technique has been embraced by various cultures and traditions over centuries and was used in ancient Egypt as a form of divination. One notable example is the use of polished metal or water vessels for scrying. Ancient Egyptians believed that such reflective surfaces could serve as portals to the spiritual realm. Individuals, often priests or seers, would gaze into these surfaces, seeking messages from the divine or insights into the future. The images or symbols perceived during scrying were interpreted as messages from the gods or as guidance for decision-making.

Crystal balls, mirrors, water surfaces, or even flames can serve as common tools for scrying. The practitioner enters a focused state of consciousness while observing their chosen medium and may receive symbolic images or messages. These visions' interpretation hinges on the intuition and spiritual sensitivity of the person performing the scrying. Scrying serves not only as a means to glimpse into the future, but also acts as an impactful tool for self-reflection and inner exploration.

To engage in scrying, start by crafting a sacred space. Select a suitable scrying tool like a crystal ball, black mirror, candle flame or reflective water surface. As you gaze into this medium, allow your mind to shift into a meditative state—let go of mundane thoughts and open yourself up to surrounding energies. Direct clear and specific questions towards the Netjeru with focus on the divine guidance you are seeking. Be attentive to any images, symbols or impressions surfacing during your session; these hold clues to sought-after answers. Trusting your intuition is key when interpreting these revelations—within these reflective depths unfolds wisdom from the Kemetic Pantheon, providing profound insights into both your spiritual journey and life path.

Pendulum Dowsing

Pendulum dowsing is a divination practice that involves the use of a pendulum—a weighted object suspended from a string or chain—to gain insights or answer questions. The practitioner holds the top end of the chain, letting the pendulum swing freely. Questions are then asked, with interpretations made based on how the pendulum moves—whether it swings back and forth, circles around, or forms other patterns. Although not explicitly linked to Kemetic spirituality, this practice can be woven into various spiritual explorations through its broader context.

1. Before use, cleanse and charge your pendulum. This can be done through methods like placing it in the light of the full moon, using sage smoke, or burying it in salt.

2. Find a serene space where you can concentrate without distractions.

Keep calm and your mind clear. Hold on to the top end of your pendulum's chain or string so it can swing without hindrance.

3. First establish a baseline by asking the pendulum for your "Yes", "No," and "Maybe" signals. For example, when engaging my pendulum, my "Yes" is a forwards and backwards movement, my "No" is a side-to-side movement, and my "Maybe" is a circular movement.

4. Next, test these signals by asking straightforward questions that have known answers; ensure the answers align with your baseline yes, no, and maybe signals.

5. After calibrating your tool this way, you're ready to ask more complex questions; just remember to keep them clear and concise so it can be answered as a yes or no. If the pendulum answers maybe or remains still, it is an indication that it either can't answer that question or it can't answer yet.

When using a pendulum for divination, it's important to handle the practice with responsibility and ethical mindfulness. As with any divination tool, there's potential for misuse. Here are some ethical considerations you should keep in mind:

- Avoid using your pendulum when emotionally or mentally unsteady (e.g., if you're stressed, angry, tired) as this could lead to inaccurate responses. To ensure that you're in the suitable mental state, consider asking your pendulum before starting: "Is now a good time to dowse?"

- Use the pendulum for positive and constructive aims. Refrain from posing questions that might inflict harm, distress, or unnecessary anxiety.

- Maintain honesty with yourself and others. If there's uncertainty about interpretation, admit it openly rather than manipulating the pendulum's responses to suit a particular narrative.

- Don't substitute medical expertise with your pendulum use—never put yourself at risk—if faced with serious health concerns, always seek professional medical help.

- Avoid using the pendulum to delve into someone else's private life without their permission—respect their privacy rights.

- When intending to use the pendulum on behalf of someone else, always ask their permission first; they should understand they have every right to decline if they wish.

- Understand the limited nature of pendulums. At times, it may be more useful to consult other forms of divination (like oracle cards, casting lots or scrying) that can provide more layered and comprehensive answers.

- Don't become dependent on pendulum dowsing. While it's a form of divination that can assist you in making decisions, it shouldn't serve as your only method for doing so.

Using a pendulum for divination taps into the subtle energies that surround us all. It serves as a powerful tool for establishing connections with deities and harnessing your own intuition. However, like any other divination tool, its interpretation is subjective—it demands trust in your instincts and developing rapport with your tool over time. Discernment and judgement are also essential; no divination tool should be used as the sole basis for making life decisions.

Dream Interpretation

Dream interpretation offers an intriguing pathway to divination in Kemetic spirituality, providing a unique window into the subconscious and spiritual messages. To maximize the benefits of this practice, start by maintaining a dream journal where you can capture all details of your dreams as soon as you wake up. Pay attention to symbols, emotions, and any recurring themes. In the

Kemetic tradition, certain symbols might hold significant meanings related to the pantheon or spiritual principles. Regularly revisit your dream journal to spot patterns and themes while seeking guidance from the symbols present. You may find it helpful to consult further resources on Kemetic symbolism to deepen your understanding. Engage in rituals, meditation, or prayer before sleep to enhance dream clarity and connection with the divine. As dreams often act as a bridge between our earthly existence and spiritual dimensions, interpreting them can yield valuable insights and messages from the Kemetic pantheon.

The topic of dream interpretation is so fascinating I've dedicated an entire bonus chapter to cover it in more detail.

***

Divination practices serve as a potent medium to commune with the deities of ancient Egypt. However, such power may sometimes be prone to misuse. It's important to remember that divination's primary purpose isn't necessarily to forecast future events—even though it's comforting to have some foresight—rather, it aims at seeking guidance from deities for personal development and societal harmony. With time and practice, you'll gradually learn how to decipher the divine wisdom that has been guiding humanity since ancient times.

An important factor to consider in the world of divination is spiritual hygiene. In Chapter 4, I provided an overview of certain practices aimed at purifying your space and yourself before delving into spiritual practices. In the following section, I'll take a closer look at this topic and offer more specific guidance related to divination.

Spiritual Hygiene Practices

"Your energy introduces you before you even speak." This quote by an unknown author captures the essence of this section. Spiritual hygiene is a basic aspect ignored by many while practicing divination, yet it holds immense significance.

Picture your spirituality like a mirror. Over time, with every interaction and experience, dust begins to accumulate on this mirror's surface, clouding its reflective abilities. Similarly, our spiritual self gathers energetic residues from our daily encounters and experiences that can skew our divine connections during divination practices if not cleansed regularly.

Spiritual hygiene revolves around regular cleansing of your energy field or aura. It helps keep your spiritual mirror polished so that the divine messages are clear and unfiltered. It also acts as a protective shield, guarding against negative energies that could distort messages received during divination.

Scientifically speaking, everything in the universe is energy vibrating at different frequencies. This includes us humans, too. Our thoughts, emotions, and actions all contribute to our personal vibrational frequency, which forms an integral part of our aura or spiritual being. A clean aura aligns better with higher frequencies, which aids clearer communication with the divine during divination practices.

Observing spiritual hygiene is a mark of respect for the sacred nature of divination tools and practices, fostering a harmonious and reverential space for the exchange of insights. Lastly, it contributes to personal well-being, promoting mental, emotional, and spiritual balance, which, in turn, enhances receptivity to intuitive insights and creates a positive environment for the divination process.

Here are some spiritual hygiene practices to follow:

- **Grounding and Centering**: Prior to any form of divination, establish a connection with the Earth's energy to ground yourself. Centering allows you to focus on the here and now.

- **Cleansing Rituals**: Make it a habit to purify your divination tools. You can do this by smudging them with sage, letting them pass through incense smoke, basking them under full moonlight, or immersing them in salt water or ocean waves.

- **Personal Cleansing**: Cleanse yourself before starting a divination session by taking a ritual bath, using essential oils, or visualizing a purifying light washing over your energy field.

- **Protection**: Create an image in your mind or perform a ritual that invokes a protective shield around you—think of it as an energetic bubble or cloak that keeps unwanted energies at bay.

- **Setting Intentions**: Be explicit about your intentions before diving into divination work; declare your openness only towards guidance that serves your highest good, and only from beings of light.

- **Meditation**: Regular meditation helps declutter the mind and boosts intuitive abilities; try weaving mindfulness practices into your daily routine.

- **Respectful Environment**: Opt for quiet spaces that exude respect when conducting divination sessions; set up an altar or sacred space that nurtures positivity and concentration.

- **Regular Energetic Clearing**: Incorporate regular practices like Reiki, aura cleansing, or other energy clearing methods into your regimen for maintaining energetic hygiene.

- **Gratitude**: Express gratitude for any guidance received during your divination sessions. This reinforces a positive and respectful connection.

- **Closing Rituals**: Once your divination session concludes, close the energy circle or ritual space. Thank any spiritual entities involved and consciously disconnect from the energies.

Remember that spiritual hygiene is a personal practice, and you may adapt these suggestions based on what resonates with you. It's important to cultivate a routine that aligns with your beliefs and enhances your spiritual well-being.

***

In conclusion, divination in Kemetic spirituality represents a sacred journey towards connecting with divine forces that shape our lives. As we delve into the rich symbolism within divination tools, it's important to remember that true magic resides in the sincerity of our connection and intentions we bring forth during these practices.

Spiritual cleanliness also becomes crucial—it's akin to ensuring a camera lens is clean for capturing pristine images. Regular cleansing rituals, prayers, and fostering a harmonious spiritual environment are key factors in guaranteeing the effectiveness of our divination efforts. May our exploration of divination lead us on a path of constant learning, growth, and an ever-deepening bond with the sacred mysteries inherent in Kemetic spirituality.

---

1. You can find these cards on Amazon at the following links: Isis Oracle Deck: https://amzn.to/3s94yuG, Auset Egyptian Oracle Cards: https://amzn.to/3OzKjOd. As an Amazon Associate I earn from qualifying purchases.

Chapter Seven

Honoring Ancestors and Ancestral Practices

"It is indeed a desirable thing to be well-descended, but the glory belongs to our ancestors." —Plutarch

Ancestral veneration, also referred to as ancestral worship, played a significant role in ancient Kemetic spirituality. So of course, it plays a significant role in modern Kemetic spirituality as well. Ancestral veneration offers a deep sense of connection with your lineage, honoring the wisdom, guidance, and spiritual presence of your ancestors.

Your ancestors do not have to be Egyptian for you to worship them as a part of your practice; no matter what culture your ancestors belonged to, you can still appreciate their knowledge and wisdom that they collected throughout the duration of their life. By engaging in ancestral practices, you have the ability to seek support, preserve cultural heritage, foster healing and reconciliation, and maintain a profound link between past, present, and future generations. Ancestor veneration is a personal and meaningful practice that should be approached with love, sincerity, and respect.

Ancestral veneration played a significant role in Kemetic spirituality because there was such an emphasis on wisdom and respecting both elders and authority figures. As a result, it was important to acknowledge the things that one's ancestors went through as a part of one's spiritual practice. By doing so, you have the opportunity to recognize the wisdom and guidance of ancestors, as well as how their experiences can influence and support your current life.

Not only is it important to honor personal ancestors, but it is important to honor ancestors of the land as well. Especially if you live in a country like the United States, the land on which you live was owned by someone centuries ago, far before you or your family got here. It is an important part of any spiritual practice to acknowledge these land-based ancestors, which also opens the door for those without any known ancestors to work with ancestral veneration as well.

Establishing a Connection with Ancestral Lineage and Heritage

One of the first important steps to take when it comes to worshipping your ancestors is to establish a connection with your ancestral lineage and heritage. It can feel hard to do this, especially if you do not really know who your ancestors are. After all, there are many reasons that you might not—including displacement, immigration, and a simple lack of historical record, and that is okay! There are still ways to work with ancestral veneration anyway.

The first step is to acknowledge the interconnectedness of the generations as well as the continuity of life. But what exactly does this entail? Well, first, you have to come to terms with the fact that regardless of if you know them, you have an ancestral lineage. Someone was born before you, and before them, and before them, and so on and so forth. Each and every generation is connected, and that does not just mean the past generations. You are also connected to the future generations that will come from you—either by creating a child of your own, adopting, or becoming a parent in a different sense.

You also have to learn to embrace the fact that life does not end just because the physical body has passed away. One concept to understand is how life and death work in tandem with each other, forming a cyclical pattern. Life does not end when you die; rather, after death, you get to go on in the afterlife, according to Kemetic cosmology. In some instances, you are reincarnated, which leads me to my next point.

It is a good idea to embrace the concept of reincarnation. The idea behind reincarnation is that once your body dies, your soul is then transferred into a different body to continue its spiritual journey on Earth. That might sound confusing, but it will become clearer as you engage with your spiritual ventures through Kemeticism. The purpose of understanding reincarnation when it comes to ancestral veneration is the mere fact that if we are reincarnated, then there is an ancestral presence walking among us on Earth. People who you might not even know can have related, soul-based lineage to you.

The next step in establishing a connection with your ancestral lineage and heritage is considering your ancestors to be sources of wisdom and guidance based on their life experiences. Your ancestors are labeled as such because they have at least one more experience on Earth than you, one more lifetime worth of experience. As such, it is important to recognize that they have therefore accumulated vast amounts of knowledge and insights that are shaped by their experiences, and they have the ability to share these insights with you.

Understand that your ancestors' experiences shape the collective consciousness. The collective consciousness is the combined body of knowledge that exists as a culmination of knowledge collected by every single person who has ever lived. Their ancestral experiences shape this body of knowledge, allowing us to be wiser overall. Comprehending this fact allows you more direct access to the body of knowledge.

Then, you must come to understand your ancestors as custodians of family and cultural traditions. Ancestors preserve and pass down cultural practices, rituals, and sacred knowledge, for instance. They remember the practices that they engaged with and share them with later generations, which leads to another thing—eventually, you, too, will have to embrace the responsibility of preserving ancestral heritage for future generations as well. It is a good idea to become acquainted with the idea of doing so. You can work to embody this concept by preparing to retain the knowledge of the spiritual practices that you encounter along your very own journey.

Furthermore, it is important to recognize your ancestors as providers of spiritual support and protection. They serve the specific role of providing you with spiritual knowledge to guide you along your journey. You should consider them to be benevolent guardians and protectors of their lineage, which means that they have it in their best interest to protect and guide you to the best of their ability.

This also means that your ancestors are there for you when it comes to times of need. In times of need, you can seek ancestral blessings and guidance through veneration practices, and it is completely okay to do so—your ancestors want to see you succeed.

The final aspect of establishing a connection with your ancestors is to explore opportunities for generational healing and reconciliation through ancestral veneration. Addressing and acknowledging ancestral wounds and traumas is something that you can absolutely do through veneration, and it is, in fact, incredibly healing. Ancestral veneration to heal personal and generational wounds or traumas can be personally transformative as well, inciting growth and development within yourself as a person as well as benefitting your lineage down the line.

It is not uncommon for people to be born with generational trauma; in fact, the field of epigenetics has proven that experiences and traumas endured by previous generations can leave a biological imprint on individuals, affecting their physical and emotional well-being throughout their lives. As such, even if nothing "bad" has happened throughout the duration of your life, it is possible to feel the remnants of ancestral trauma reverberating through your spirit. Ancestral veneration is one way to break through this, creating healing and restoring harmony between yourself, your ancestors, and generations to come.

Ancestral Veneration Rituals, Practices, and Offerings

Diving into the world of ancestral veneration rituals, practices, and offerings can equip you with everything that you need in order to engage in ancestral worship in a way that is both respectful and mutually beneficial. Let's explore some of the methods of doing so.

Ancestral Altars

One of the things that you can do to get started with ancestor veneration is to create ancestral altars to serve as a focal point for veneration and connection. Remember how we set up an altar earlier in the book for your general practices? You can do the same thing to set up a dedicated ancestral altar, which would serve as a designated space where you engage with spiritual work connecting you to your ancestors. Your ancestral altar can be within its own dedicated space in your home, or you can include it in the same sacred space as your initial altar.

Ancestral altars are significant in that they serve as sacred spaces for veneration. Taking the time to dedicate a specific space to the act of worship is something mystical, something moving. The very dedication of a space to your ancestors is a devotional act, and that space itself thus becomes a location wherein you can worship your ancestors. You should consider the altar to be a physical representation of the spiritual connection that you have with your ancestors. It is a location where you worship, connect, talk to, and make offerings to your ancestors. It is, in essence, a central location wherein you can devote energies specifically to your ancestors, which makes it a special place unlike any other.

An important component of building an altar for your ancestors is selecting appropriate locations and materials for doing so. I recommend opting for an indoor location for an ancestor altar simply because it is not something that you will want to carry with you or move around a lot. Select a peaceful and respectful location for the altar, one that is perhaps a little bit private and in a place that is uplifting. You can even ask your ancestors to tell you where they would like their altar built and then walk around your home until a certain space resonates. The best materials for an ancestral altar are wood, stone, and metal, and every material should have symbolic significance.

Then, you can select meaningful symbols that represent your ancestors and their legacy. Things like their favorite flowers, photos of them, and small trinkets that they owned while living if you have them, are excellent options for decorating your altar. You should also include any spiritual tools that you use for ancestor veneration. If you know of something that is particularly meaningful to your ancestors—like a symbol, animal, or deity—then you can absolutely include something pertaining to that on your altar. You should also make considerations for offerings. Among the most popular offerings are food, water and other liquids, candles, incense, and other meaningful items. You can even have a designated spot on the altar, whereupon your ancestors know that something is for them.

Once you have an altar or dedicated working space for ancestral veneration, you can begin to make offerings to your ancestors. The point of these offerings is to let them know that you appreciate them and their legacy and that you recognize that they are doing their absolute best to help you. Offerings energize ancestors the same as they energize deities, meaning that offerings are always appreciated and helpful when it comes to ensuring that they can continue to provide support.

There are many different types of offerings that you can provide to your ancestors, which can include food and symbolic objects that represent your ancestors and their legacy. You can include their favorite foods, drinks, and items on the altar, as well as things that they cherished in their life. It is truly up to you what you decide to offer, but it should always be something meaningful in some way—your offerings should have symbolic significance, and you should understand that significance. Furthermore, you should understand that offerings represent a gesture of respect and gratitude.

Offerings can be made on the altar, either in a bowl or chalice or some other container. For food and drink offerings, be sure to discard the offering before it rots to avoid flies, smells, or any disrespectful energies.

Finally, it is important to exercise regular maintenance as well as care for your ancestral altar. Life gets busy, that is for sure, but it is a classic sign of respect to keep your altar clear from dust and debris for your ancestors. Regularly replenishing offerings as well as maintaining the sacred space with a degree of reverence is important too.

Prayers and Invocations

Another thing that you can do to practice ancestor veneration is to recite prayers and invocations. Prayers and invocations are valuable ways to invite ancestral presence and guidance into your life. They signify to your ancestors that you want to talk, as well as that you acknowledge their role and aid in your life. You can use traditional invocations or prayers to invoke ancestral spirits by looking up common prayers, especially ones used in pagan and Kemetic circles. But if pre-made prayers are not your thing, it is perfectly valid—and in some situations, even more desirable—to compose your own prayers. Composing a heartfelt prayer or invocation is a wonderful idea to connect directly with your ancestors.

Furthermore, you should make it a habit to pray or communicate with your ancestors regularly. A regular consultation between you and them is excellent, because it keeps an open line of dialogue between you and your ancestors. Praying or even speaking to them daily can be a great way to establish regular practice, which you should make time to do with any spirits you work with. An example of an invocation you can use is as follows:

> *"I call upon the spirits of my ancestors, those who walked before me in the sands of time.*
>
> *I invite you to be here with me now as I seek your protection, love, and healing.*
>
> *Please guide me on my sacred path. Please show me the way.*
>
> *Thank you, thank you, thank you."*

Rituals and Ceremonies

Rituals and ceremonies are another good way to recognize and appreciate your ancestors. For example, you can observe annual festivals or special occasions that are dedicated to ancestral veneration. You can even celebrate your ancestors on holidays or their birthday if you do not follow a celebration calendar in a spiritual sense. Moreover, you can participate in communal rituals, which will strengthen the ancestral bond within the community. This is particularly nice when it comes to the matter of land ancestors.

If you do not celebrate holidays and you are not sure when your ancestors were born or what dates were notable to them, then you can always designate remembrance days of your own. This will give you the opportunity to commemorate ancestors and honor their memory on specific days that you select yourself. During these days, you can pray, make offerings, and reflect on the lessons and contributions that your ancestors have made.

Researching Family History

It might be obvious, but you can also work to engage with your ancestors by conducting family history and genealogical research in order to deepen the connection that you have with your ancestors. You can look into your family history in specific, or you can research your genealogy to find a more overarching lineage that designates your ancestral roots. This will allow you to research countries, traditions, and practices that play a role in your ancestry. In addition, this allows you to uncover ancestral stories that enhance your sense of ancestral identity as well.

Acts of Service

Engaging in acts of community service or charity is a good way to honor your ancestors, especially if you engage in these acts of goodwill in their name. Community service acts and acts of charity are the perfect way to honor your ancestors' virtues and values. These actions allow you to embody the virtues of your ancestors through direct demonstrations of kindness and compassion, which then also makes the world a better place, you a better person, and aligns you with the principles of Ma'at.

Embracing Cultural Practices

Finally, you can embrace cultural traditions and practices in order to preserve your cultural and ancestral heritage. This involves participating in culture festivals, ceremonies, and practices to honor your ancestral traditions. This helps you both keep your current ancestral traditions alive, as well as teaches these traditions to younger individuals who are interested in learning as well. Remember that this is part of your role as a cultural steward, carrying your ancestral practices with you for generations to come just like your ancestors did.

Ancestral Healing and Reconciliation

Ancestral healing and reconciliation is another valuable part of ancestral work. It involves recognizing ancestral wounds, traumas, and unresolved issues that can impact the present. Acknowledging the impact of past experiences on the present and future generations is an important aspect of ancestral healing, and you can contribute something unique in terms of healing and growth for you, your ancestors, and future generations to come. It is also a good idea to understand that unhealed ancestral wounds can impact individual and collective well-being. As we learned previously when we touched on the topic of epigenetics, even if something did not happen to you directly, unhealed wounds that your ancestors have could contribute significantly to how you feel in modern times.

One thing that you can do to work toward ancestral healing and reconciliation is to honor your ancestors by acknowledging that the experiences of their past have impacted your lineage. In other words, recognize the fact that your ancestors' experiences were both meaningful and impactful, and you have already made great strides in your ancestor work. Engaging in rituals and practices to honor and remember these ancestors—the ones who have endured these challenges in specific—is a good way to do so. You can also offer up prayers and/or invocations for the healing and uplifting of ancestral spirits, letting them know that you recognize the hardships that they have endured.

After that, it is a good idea to move forward with some healing practices that are able to address ancestral wounds and promote harmony. Some of the spiritual healing techniques, as explored in the section *How to Connect with Yourself* in Chapter 4, will not only contribute to your present well-being, but can also simultaneously energetically release ancestral traumas and pain. If needed, you can also reach out to spiritual guides and deities for assistance—they will be more than willing to help with the facilitation of ancestral healing.

Rituals, meditation, and forgiveness as tools for ancestral healing are quite common. You can perform forgiveness rituals, for instance, to release and transmute ancestral burdens. If your ancestors have harmed someone or been harmed by someone, especially if they are harboring negative feelings about the experience, this type of ritual can be especially helpful. Meditation and inner work can help you foster inner understanding and compassion for your ancestors, allowing you to understand what they feel and why with more depth.

The purpose of all of this is not just to benefit your ancestors, though. It is also a transformative effort that has power over current and future generations. For example, ancestral healing can provide healing to you or someone in your family as well, which can contribute to more beneficial dynamics between you and other people—including your family. This may be particularly useful if you have a rather rocky family history. What's more is that embracing the potential for ancestral healing can create a positive ripple effect within society, which is part of what Kemetic spirituality is all about.

The Guidance and Wisdom of Ancestors

Working with ancestors has a point to it—or a few points, at least. One of the points of following ancestral practices is reveling in their guidance and wisdom, which involves harnessing a few skills in order to be able to utilize your learnings. First, it is important to understand how ancestral guidance is both received and communicated. One way that ancestral messages are communicated is through dreams, which means that if you hope to be aligned with your ancestors, you should work on dream analysis. Honing your intuition is useful as well, as intuitive messages are also going to come through. And while not everything is going to be a sign, it is definitely not a bad idea to keep an eye out for signs along your journey. Particularly, take note of animal sightings, angel numbers (many of the same number repeating themselves), and anything else out of the ordinary. Once again, it is necessary to embrace the idea that your ancestral spirits are benevolent and protective.

On the subject of intuition, being able to connect with your intuition is going to be instrumental. Your ancestors will send you messages through intuitive connections, and being able to actually receive those messages is important. In order to really boost your intuition, you will need to trust your intuitive senses and inner guidance when it comes to seeking ancestral counsel. This means that you cannot let second-guessing yourself get in the way of your ability to receive messages. Furthermore, you should practice speaking with your ancestors regularly so that you are in the habit of receiving these messages, thus ensuring that you do not miss something vital due to not paying attention.

In addition, you can actively seek the counsel of your ancestors through dream work, visions, and divinatory practices, such as those I outlined in the previous chapter. For example, analyzing what comes up as a result of dreams and meditations can reveal to you hidden messages, and divination work can allow you to directly encounter those messages. For newcomers exploring divination, a pendulum—a suspended object that freely swings to convey messages—is a beginner-friendly option. Various online tutorials can guide you through its usage. However, it's crucial to approach these powerful tools with respect and caution, acknowledging the reality of energy dynamics. Oracle and tarot cards are another good option for interpreting messages from ancestors, although they require a bit more research and interpretation. If you are up for the challenge, I do recommend it.

As you receive this ancestral wisdom, it is important that you learn to navigate the challenges that life presents you—as well as to make informed decisions—utilizing what you have learned throughout your work. Applying ancestral wisdom involves seeking guidance from ancestors when facing important life choices and decisions. This means using the knowledge that your ancestors have to guide you. Remember that everything they have lived through, generations before, you have lived through as well. Drawing on this wisdom to gain insight and perspectives on various situations is a good idea as well, allowing you to more fully analyze a situation.

Finally, it is important to embrace the role of your ancestors as supportive allies and protectors on your spiritual path. Remember that your ancestors are always there for you. Like Netjeru, they benefit from your involvement with them, and they are willing to provide guidance in return as well. It is okay to consult them for anything that you need or any advice you'd like to hear. Understand that your ancestors are friends and not foes—even when they tell you things you might not want to hear. Always keep in mind that you can invoke their assistance and guidance during spiritual practices and rituals as well.

Ancestral Veneration and Personal Growth

Ancestral veneration has significant impacts on personal growth, and it is a good idea to be able to understand the transformative potential of this relationship. The ancestral connection has the ability to positively impact your life in many ways, and this includes the elements of self-awareness and empowerment. Through listening to our ancestors, we can become more aware of things like right and wrong in the world, what appropriate actions are, and how we can become better people, for instance. With our ancestors walking along by our sides, we feel more empowered to act in ways that we know are just because who better to guide us than our own family, spiritual or otherwise? Ancestral veneration is something that can be embraced as a catalyst for inner growth and spiritual development in this way.

It is important that as you use the gifts offered by your ancestors that you do not take anything for granted. Cultivating a sense of gratitude and reverence for the gifts and blessings of our ancestors is the perfect way to show that we appreciate what they do for us, no matter how big or small that may be. You can do this by practicing daily expressions of gratitude to honor their support. Something as small as a short prayer, offering up the first sip of your morning coffee, or performing a short ritual can be a good way to extend this gratitude. As you progress throughout your day, ensure that you're doing what you can to recognize the role that your ancestors played in shaping the present and the future alike.

In order to continue to grow using what our ancestors have to offer, you have to be willing to integrate ancestral teachings and values into both your daily life and your spiritual practices. This means embodying ancestral virtues and values as a means of personal and spiritual alignment. For example, you can do this by being sure to offer kindness and compassion toward others, perpetuating that same characteristic that your ancestors would want you to. You can also employ the wisdom offered by ancestors to update your spiritual rituals, prayers, and affirmations, gaining more and more from your spiritual endeavors as a result.

Embracing the interconnectedness of the past, present, and future through ancestral veneration is useful as well. You're going to want to recognize the fact that, at its core and truest nature, the ancestral connection is timeless. It does not have a limitation or boundary on it, making it something else that is eternal within Kemeticism. Ancestral worship and veneration exist far beyond the bounds of temporal restrictions, and it is important to recognize the empowerment and strength that you can gain from these timeless connections as well. The continuum of life allows us to benefit from the support and encouragement that ancestral spirits are willing to offer.

In all, ancestor veneration is one of the key aspects of Kemetic practice. Acknowledging the ongoing support and guidance from ancestors is vital, and I encourage you to explore the empowerment offered by ancestral veneration.

Chapter Eight

Sacred Texts and Wisdom of Egypt

"True teaching is not an accumulation of knowledge; it is an awakening of consciousness which goes through successive stages."
—Ancient Egyptian Proverb

As we continue our journey into Kemetic spirituality, let's uncover some of the secrets surrounding sacred texts and the wisdom of Egypt. The sacred texts and wisdom of Egypt—particularly the Book of the Dead and the Pyramid Texts—are among the most valuable Kemetic resources that one can delve into. They offer profound insights regarding beliefs about the afterlife, the divine realm, and the individual spiritual journey on which we all embark. Exploring these texts empowers you with valuable knowledge about both ancient Egyptian culture and spirituality. Moreover, doing so offers insights that you can apply to your modern interpretations of Kemetic spirituality.

Additionally, the wisdom provided by literature, proverbs, and the teachings of ancient Egypt offers timeless guidance on how we can live a life that is virtuous, harmonious, and balanced within ourselves and the community around us.

The Funerary Texts

Funerary texts were prevalent in ancient Egypt due to the importance the Egyptians placed on the afterlife and the journey of the soul beyond death. The ancient Egyptians believed in an intricate and complex concept of the afterlife, and funerary texts were instrumental in guiding the deceased through the challenges and transitions they would face in the realm of the dead. The Book of the Dead and the Pyramid Texts are two of the most significant ancient Egyptian religious funerary texts. The Coffin Texts, though lesser known, are considered a continuation and elaboration of the religious ideas found in the Pyramid Texts.

Each text offers valuable insight regarding the beliefs, rituals, and concepts surrounding death, the afterlife, and the divine. For anyone who hopes to become a skilled practitioner and a knowledgeable spiritual being, understanding these texts is essential. All three texts are crucial to one's understanding of spiritual beliefs and practices found with ancient Egypt, offering unique perspectives on the perceptions that they had regarding both the afterlife and the role of Pharaohs within the divine realm.

The Book of the Dead

Compiled during the New Kingdom (c. 1550–1070 BCE) period of ancient Egypt, the Book of the Dead is a compilation of funerary texts. It consists of various spells, rituals, and hymns, all of which were either written on papyrus scrolls or inscribed upon the walls of burial chambers. The texts compiled in the Book of the Dead were intended to assist the deceased in their journey throughout the afterlife, making sure that they experienced a successful transition to the realm of Osiris—who, as you know, is the god of the afterlife and the dead.

There are many themes and concepts that are central to the Book of the Dead—topics explored that round out the book and make it worth exploring.

One such concept that you are already familiar with is Ma'at, which makes itself a central theme of the Book of the Dead. Ma'at within this book represents the principle of cosmic order alongside balance and truth. According to the ancient Egyptians, living in alignment with Ma'at was crucial to the success of one's afterlife journey. In other words, they believed that to have a satisfactory afterlife, life must be spent living according to Ma'at.

The afterlife journey is another key concept explored within the Book of the Dead. Inside this book are spells and instructions that can be utilized to guide the deceased through various journeys, challenges, and obstacles that will be encountered within the afterlife—because challenges do not solely exist within the living realm. When someone dies, they are meant to use the Book of the Dead to help them navigate. This is why it contains mentions of encounters with deities, maps of the journey, judgment scenes within the hall of Ma'at, weighing the heart against Ma'at, and more.

Finally, protection and guidance are explored within the Book of the Dead. Some of the spells within the Book of the Dead are intended to protect the dead against malevolent—or negative—forces. They are also intended to provide the dead with the knowledge, power, and skills necessary to navigate the afterlife successfully.

The Pyramid Texts

The other valuable ancient text that we have is the Pyramid Texts. Initially, the Pyramid Texts were created with the explicit intention of assisting a deceased Pharaoh in ascending to the afterlife. It was believed that this text would help them do so in order to join the company with the gods because, if you remember, Pharaohs were ancient Egypt's way of linking the mystical world to the world on earth. Initially, the Pyramid Texts were aptly named as such because they were carved into the walls of pyramids that belonged to rulers in the Old Kingdom (c. 2686–2181 BCE). Moreover, the Pyramid Texts are some of the oldest religious writings that we have from Egypt.

Much like the Book of the Dead, the Pyramid Texts also have a few central themes to take note of. For instance, the Pharaoh's journey is a major concept that the Pyramid Texts explore. The Pyramid Texts explore the journey that a deceased Pharaoh would embark upon in the afterlife. During this journey, it is said that a Pharaoh would then be transformed into a divine being and united with the gods as a sort of reward for the divine purpose they served on Earth. In fact, the Pyramid Texts explicitly emphasize this connection—the one between the Pharaoh and the divine—due to their role as an intermediary on Earth.

Similarly, the Pyramid Texts talk about the divine connection that Pharaohs have with the divine. It really emphasizes this connection due to two reasons. Chiefly among them is the fact that it recognizes the role that Pharaohs played on Earth, with the other reason being that this text was intended to be predominantly used by Pharaohs to guide them after death. The third main concept emphasized within the Pyramid Texts involves rituals and offerings. Within the texts are rituals, spells, and offerings that help the Pharaoh transition to the afterlife and secure their much-deserved divine status.

The Coffin Texts

The Coffin Texts are a collection of ancient Egyptian funerary spells and religious teachings, primarily inscribed on coffins and sarcophagi during the Middle Kingdom (c. 2055–1650 BCE). These texts were designed to guide and protect the deceased in their journey through the afterlife, providing a comprehensive guide to ensure a successful transition to the realm of the dead. The Coffin Texts represent an evolution from earlier funerary practices, such as the Pyramid Texts, and reflect a broader accessibility to religious teachings beyond the elite class.

The texts encompass a wide range of themes, including spells for protection, guidance through the various stages of the afterlife, and invocations to deities associated with death and rebirth. Unlike the Pyramid Texts, which were exclusively reserved for the pharaohs, the Coffin Texts were available to a broader segment of society, often inscribed on the coffins of high-ranking officials and members of the aristocracy. This democratization of religious knowledge reflects a shift in religious beliefs towards a more inclusive approach.

The Coffin Texts delve into intricate details about the soul's journey, describing the challenges and obstacles faced in the afterlife and providing magical formulas and incantations to overcome these challenges. Similar to the Book of the Dead, the texts emphasize the importance of Ma'at, the ancient Egyptian concept of cosmic balance and order, and the adherence to moral principles in both earthly and afterlife existence. The texts also contain references to various deities, such as Osiris, Anubis, and Hathor, who play essential roles in the judgment of the deceased and their eventual rebirth.

While the Coffin Texts share similarities with the Pyramid Texts, they are more extensive in scope and complexity. They mark an important phase in the development of ancient Egyptian religious thought, influencing subsequent funerary literature like the Book of the Dead. As a crucial source of information on ancient Egyptian beliefs about death and the afterlife, the Coffin Texts offer valuable insights into the religious and spiritual dimensions of this ancient civilization.

All three of these texts—the Book of the Dead, the Pyramid Texts and the Coffin Texts—serve to reflect the widely held ancient Egyptian belief in the way that life continues after death, as well as the importance of success in the journey that one embarks upon in the afterlife. Through these texts, ancient Egyptians and spiritualists alike sought to navigate the complicated realms of the afterlife, attain divine status, and maintain harmony with Ma'at even after life ended. These texts offer valuable insight into the rich religious culture of ancient Egypt.

Wisdom Literature, Proverbs, and Teachings

The wisdom literature, proverbs, and teachings extend far beyond the two texts that I previously mentioned, including instructional texts and more. Understanding these foundational texts is essential for navigating Kemetic history.

Instructional Texts

Instructional texts were one of many forms of wisdom literature in ancient Egypt. They were perhaps the most prominent form of wisdom literature during this time and in this place, and they served as a guide for ethical and moral behavior—both things that were of the essence in ancient Egypt.

Instructions of Ptahhotep

One of the most renowned examples is the "Instructions of Ptahhotep" writing, which, as you can guess, is said to have been written by Ptahhotep. Ptahhotep was a high-ranked official during the Fifth Dynasty of the Old Kingdom. In this text, there are various maxims and teachings that Ptahhotep offered to his son directly—although we still have much to glean from the texts today. It emphasizes the importance of respecting superiors one has, displaying humility, and adhering to a code of ethical conduct in all aspects of life.

The "Instructions of Ptahhotep" covers a wide array of topics, including anything from advice on proper behavior within a court setting all the way to the importance of learning from others and respecting the wisdom that elders have to offer us. This work emphasizes virtues like self-control, patience, and honesty as well. Much like other texts in the instructional genre, this text aimed to provide guidance on how to live a just and fulfilling life.

So why am I telling you about this text? Well, it is still applicable to our modern lives today. While all elements of ancient wisdom are not going to apply to the modern world, the "Instructions of Ptahhotep" contains key information that we can still apply to our world today. This is particularly useful for the modern Kemetic practitioner because a major part of practicing Kemetic spirituality involves ethical conduct, like abiding by the principles of Ma'at. Ergo, the "Instructions of Ptahhotep" can also be employed to help a modern Kemetic practitioner live by a just moral code, even today.

Ancient Egyptian Proverbs

Another important text from ancient Egypt—or rather, a category of texts—is ancient Egyptian proverbs. Proverbs held significant meaning in ancient Egypt due to their striking ability to encapsulate profound wisdom within the scope of a concise yet memorable saying. The succinct expressions of knowledge offered by proverbs were often passed down from one generation to the next, therefore reflecting both the cultural values of ancient Egypt as well as the accumulated experiences of the society as a whole. The proverbs were originally passed around through oral tradition—spoken to one another, then memorized and spoken yet again—and eventually, they were recorded on papyri and tomb walls.

Ancient Egyptian proverbs were very distinct in their nature. Some of the characteristics of these proverbs included vivid imagery, metaphors, and parallel structures—sentence phrasing meant to indicate emphasis. Intrinsically, ancient Egyptian proverbs were very simple, and this simplicity made sure that proverbs were accessible to all manner of social classes within Egypt. Even those who were illiterate could understand the wisdom shared by proverbs, which was definitely a major benefit of passing wisdom through these phrases. Common themes focused on by proverbs included the importance of hard work, the value of wisdom, the transitory nature of life, and the consequences of one's actions.

Much like the "Instructions of Ptahhotep," ancient Egyptian proverbs play a role in how modern Kemetic practitioners do what they do best today. Not only do these proverbs highlight unique facets of ancient Egyptian society, but they imbue modern practitioners with the ability to follow moral codes and ethical structures that are in line with Ma'at, allowing for the use of Heka and work with

Netjeru to be more fruitful and fulfilling on a personal level. Even the simplest of proverbs have something to offer us!

Teachings of Amenemope

The next works that I want to talk about that were prevalent within ancient Egypt are the "Teachings of Amenemope" and the "Maxims of Ptahhotep." Within ancient Egypt, and especially during the New Kingdom period, Amenemope was considered to be a sage—a very wise person from whom wisdom could be drawn. In his work, the "Teachings of Amenemope," there are myriad similarities between it and the biblical Book of Proverbs. Within the text, there are approximately thirty chapters, and each chapter contains ethical teachings as well as practical advice for the reader to live a just life.

There are many themes within the "Teachings of Amenemope," including an emphasis on humility, self-control, and respect for authority—which, as you can probably tell, was essential in ancient Egypt. The "Teachings of Amenemope" encourages those who read it to avoid arrogance and demonstrate kindness, as well as compassion and generosity, toward others. The teachings within this work focus on virtues like honesty, integrity, prudence, and more, with the aim of instilling good moral values and character within the reader.

This is another work that can be instrumental for a modern practitioner. Offering actionable and practical advice alike, this transformative and time-tested work allows modern practitioners to see what values were prime among the ancient Egyptians, thus allowing modern practitioner to develop their own moral code based on the initiatives set in ancient Egypt. Moreover, the "Teachings of Amenemope" offers sage advice regarding how one can live in accordance with Ma'at—even if it does not explicitly state that this is the goal of the work.

Maxims of Ptahhotep

Similarly, there are the "Maxims of Ptahhotep," which, as you can guess, are attributed to the very same Ptahhotep that we talked about earlier. The "Maxims of Ptahhotep" is another significant text within the body of wisdom literature from ancient Egypt. Collected within this work are various ethical teachings and advice for maintaining social order and harmony. Ptahhotep stresses in his work the importance of humility and modesty, reminding readers that success and prosperity should not lead to arrogance or neglect of one's duties.

If the "Teachings of Amenemope" teach an individual about their own importance of embodying certain traits, then the "Maxims of Ptahhotep" serve to indicate more societal rules and structures that are important as well. To a modern practitioner, this text can be used to help navigate some of the more societally based aspects of Kemetic spirituality. Remember when we discussed Ma'at, how there was an emphasis on societally acting well, too—treating others with respect, kindness, and empathy, for example? This is one such text that can serve as a guiding light.

Dialogue of a Man with His Soul

The last text that I want to talk about is the "Dialogue of a Man with His Soul," which is a remarkable piece of wisdom literature found in the Papyrus Chester Beatty IX, dating to the New Kingdom period. This particular text serves as a thought-provoking introspection wherein the protagonist engages in a conversation with his own soul, as the title would suggest. Readers get to oversee this inner dialogue that occurs between the man and his soul, observing how the dialogue itself models the individual's struggles, fears, and doubts about life, death, and morality.

Through the dialogue presented in the text, the protagonist seeks to attain spiritual growth and align his actions with Ma'at. The text emphasizes the importance of self-awareness, acknowledging one's imperfections, and striving to live in harmony with the divine order. Modern practitioners can take notes from this book as to how to align themselves with spiritual growth and Ma'at, furthering their own spiritual journey.

In all, wisdom literature, proverbs, and teachings in ancient Egypt played a significant role in guiding individuals to live virtuous, ethical, and balanced lives. These texts conveyed practical advice, ethical principles, and philosophical insights that were cherished by the ancient Egyptians as essential aspects of a harmonious and just society. The enduring wisdom of these literary works continues to offer valuable lessons for modern readers, inspiring contemplation and reflection on the timeless themes of human existence.

Spiritual Insights and Guidance

As we begin to close off our journey together, there is an array of spiritual insight and guidance that I'd like to share with you—including things that I've learned myself, as well as things that other practitioners like me have explored. Let's talk a bit more about Ma'at, as well as other spiritual aspects to help you grow.

Embracing Ma'at and Living in Balance

As you know from your existing journey with Kemetic spirituality, Ma'at is the principle of cosmic order, truth, and harmony in ancient Egyptian spirituality. Ma'at is emphasized both within the practices of individuals throughout ancient Egypt, as well as in some of the wisdom literature and other texts that we've discussed previously. Living in alignment with Ma'at is one of the most important aspects of a strong spiritual journey guided by wisdom and integrity.

Living in alignment with Ma'at includes many things, but chiefly among them is practicing ethical behavior as well as maintaining balance. Balance is perhaps one of the most important concepts, demonstrating how it is important to have our thoughts, actions, and emotions working in tandem with one another. Embracing Ma'at fosters a greater sense of purpose and fulfillment that can carry you throughout your spiritual journey, indicating the strides you have made within your practice. Moreover, embracing Ma'at allows you to contribute directly to the greater harmony of the universe in an obvious, clear way.

In all, it is important to remember that there are essential aspects as well as benefits of living in alignment and balance with Ma'at. Among those aspects are honesty, justice, and respect toward others as well as toward nature. If you can keep these few things in mind as you progress throughout your spiritual journey, other lessons will follow. These lessons will allow you to contribute to yourself, your community, and the universe in a truly meaningful way.

Recognizing the Divinity Within Each Individual

Another important spiritual lesson that I had to learn involved recognizing the divinity that lies within each individual. The ancient Egyptians, for instance, believed that every single individual possessed a divine essence within them. This keeps itself in alignment with the idea of interconnectedness—that we are not so different from the gods and goddesses we worship. It is important to recognize this divine spark within yourself as well as within others.

Recognizing the divine spark in yourself and others is no small task; it invites so much positivity into the world, including a nurturing sense of compassion, empathy, and a sense of interconnectedness unlike any other. Even just acknowledging the fact that we are all divine beings is a huge step in the right direction for any spiritual practitioner.

Part of recognizing this divine spark is treating others with kindness and respect. It is not enough to simply say to yourself, "Okay, everyone is divine." Rather, you have to take the step to treat everybody with both kindness and respect, as this is the best way to acknowledge the divineness within us as well as the sacredness of human life. Human life is just that—sacred—and Kemetic spiritual practitioners make it a point to respect that.

Overall, understanding the divinity within each of us encourages a deeper appreciation for the diversity and worth of all souls. While some people choose not to live their lives with the guidance of an ethical and moral code, it is important to recognize that that is their right, and it is a part of their own spiritual journey, even if they decline to have one. Regardless of someone's beliefs, feelings, and attitudes, extending them baseline kindness and respect shows that you truly value human life and the soul.

Understanding the Unity of the Cosmos

In addition, you have to understand the unity of the cosmos. Ancient Egyptians believed that the universe was a unified whole that was governed by cosmic forces. In other words, they believed that the universe was one cohesive thing that was all under the control of cosmic forces—such as Heka, for example. Part of recognizing this fact is also recognizing the interdependence and interconnectedness of all aspects of life. Everything truly is connected, no matter how far out you look. Understanding this interconnectedness and interdependence allows you to foster respect and appreciation for the universe and everything in it.

Appreciating the unity of the cosmos fosters reverence for the natural world and its cycles. From moon cycles to planetary rotations, we come to appreciate the natural world and everything in it as we realize that everything is interconnected. The interconnectedness of all living beings allows us to develop a profound sense of spiritual connection, which is beneficial. It allows us to see the role that we play in spirituality, as well as contextualizes our existence to an extent. When you look up to space, everything out there can feel so far away. But the reality of the situation is that the stars, the planets, the sun and moon, the tides of the ocean, and even the change of the seasons are all part of us because we belong to the same beautiful natural world. This realization is a profound one, allowing you to realize all the ways in which Heka is embodied throughout the cosmos.

Cultivating Virtues for Personal Growth

Another aspect of your spiritual journey is cultivating virtues for personal growth. Spiritual growth involves the cultivation of virtues in order to elevate your character and consciousness. In other words, you have to develop skills, morals, and ethics that make you a better person and align you more closely with your higher self. Virtues like humility, compassion, integrity, wisdom, patience, and gratitude are highly valued within spiritual circles, which means that these are the primary virtues you should strive to attain.

By attaining virtues, you become a better version of yourself—one who is able to embody the principles of Ma'at in everyday life. This makes you a more balanced individual, as well as leads to a sense of purpose and fulfillment because of the opportunity to align your life with higher spiritual principles.

As you navigate both spirituality and your personal life, it is a good idea to try your best to cultivate virtues like the ones that I just mentioned. Not only do these virtues more closely align you with Ma'at and therefore influence you spiritually, but they also contribute significantly to your success as a person. As a person, these virtues allow you to interact with others more peacefully and respectfully, facilitating respectful relationships as well.

Viewing Life as a Spiritual Journey

The final piece of spiritual advice that I have for you is to view life as a spiritual journey. The ancient Egyptians viewed life as an ongoing spiritual journey that did not end just because someone's life on Earth ended. In other words, they perceived life to be a never-ending journey that led from worldly life into the afterlife, with the way you lived on Earth influencing how you live within the afterlife. It was believed that the part of us that continued on after death was the immortal soul—which continued to carry on our spiritual journey after our physical body passed away.

This understanding honed by the ancient Egyptians encouraged a deeper appreciation for the present moment and making meaningful choices. While they believed we live on immortality, our life on Earth is a gift and, as such, should be appreciated. Every moment is sacred and should be viewed as such. Viewing life as a spiritual journey inspires personal growth, seeking wisdom and positive contributions to the world. This means that understanding spirituality's role in your journey makes a world of difference.

By integrating these spiritual insights and guidance into their lives, individuals can find greater meaning, purpose, and a sense of interconnectedness with the larger tapestry of existence. Ancient Egyptian wisdom continues to inspire seekers today, encouraging a harmonious way of living, ethical conduct, and a profound reverence for the sacredness of life's journey.

Chapter Nine

Symbolism and Sacred Arts

"Symbolism is the language of the Mysteries. By symbols, men have ever sought to talk to each other those thoughts which transcend the limitations of language." —Manly P. Hall

As we conclude our exploration of Kemetic spirituality, we delve into a captivating realm that enriches our understanding even further: symbolism and sacred arts. These elements served as intricate threads weaving through the tapestry of ancient Egyptian spirituality, offering valuable insights into their beliefs and practices. Symbolism and sacred arts were not merely superficial embellishments, but rather gateways to deeper dimensions of connection with the divine. By delving into the intricate meanings behind symbols and the significance of various artistic expressions, we gain a glimpse into how ancient Egyptians sought to bridge the earthly and spiritual realms.

Throughout this journey, we've uncovered the guiding principles of Ma'at, connected with the pantheon of deities, explored ancestral veneration, and deciphered the wisdom of ancient texts. Now, we step into a new chapter that unveils how symbolism served as a language of the soul, allowing the ancient Egyptians to communicate with the gods, understand the cosmic order, and tap into the mystical forces that shape existence. The sacred arts, including hieroglyphs, sculptures, paintings, music, and dance, acted as conduits of spiritual energy, enabling practitioners to enter altered states of consciousness, connect with the divine, and experience the its mysteries firsthand.

By delving into the symbolism and sacred arts of Kemetic spirituality, we gain a deeper appreciation for the holistic nature of their spiritual practices. We'll explore the significance of well-known symbols like the Ankh, the Scarab, and the Djed Pillar, uncovering their hidden meanings and their role in guiding the spiritual journey. Moreover, we'll discover how art and music were not merely aesthetic pursuits but powerful tools for invoking divine presence, storytelling, and engaging in rituals that connected the mundane and the divine.

So, as we embark on this final chapter, let's journey into the realm of symbolism and sacred arts in Kemetic spirituality. Let's unravel the threads that wove together the fabric of their beliefs and practices, and in doing so, deepen our own connection to the timeless wisdom that continues to inspire and guide us today.

The Role and Significance of Hieroglyphs

Let's start out with the role and significance of hieroglyphs as they were utilized in ancient Egypt. You may know hieroglyphs as the symbols that trace along the sides of pyramids and inside funeral tombs, for example. Did you know that hieroglyphs were actually an ancient system of writing that was revered and very valuable within individual cultures? Hieroglyphs were a system of writing that was used primarily by the ancient Egyptians, and the system of writing utilized pictorial symbols alongside phonetic elements to comprise an entirely unique written language. Hieroglyphs played a vital role in writings that were valued in Egyptian society, including religious, historical, and administrative documents. Hieroglyphs were utilized to record important events, prayers, hymns, rituals, and so much more, playing just as valuable a role in Egyptian society as written English plays in our lives today.

However, hieroglyphs were a bit more significant and sacred than English is to us because the ancient Egyptians believed that hieroglyphs were sacred and believed to possess magical powers. The ancient Egyptians believed that hieroglyphs were capable of conveying divine messages and preserving knowledge for eternity. In fact, hieroglyphs were used as spiritual conduits between humans and gods, and they are more than just symbolic representations, they are vibrational energies encapsulated in visual form. Science has shown us that everything in the universe vibrates at different frequencies – including words and thoughts. This concept was well understood by our ancient Egyptian ancestors who used these symbolic images encoded with specific vibrations to communicate with the divine realm.

The sacred significance of hieroglyphs to ancient Egyptians is most evident when considering the term "Medu Neter", the ancient Egyptian designation for what we currently identify as hieroglyphs. Medu Neter means "divine words", "divine speech", or "divine language", a title that clearly emphasizes the sacred nature of this script.

Figure 2: Hierogylphs (Medu Neter)

Picture this: A bird soaring high in the sky against the backdrop of radiant sunlight - such an image would symbolize 'freedom' or 'ascension' universally across cultures. That's precisely how hieroglyphs work; they tap into universal archetypes and meanings embedded deep within our collective consciousness.

This meant that the use of hieroglyphs as a method of written language was even more valuable than we can perhaps perceive it to be today. The ability to read and write in this language was considered to be prestigious, and as a result, only scribes and priests typically had the ability to read and write in this language. However, this was a valuable role in that priests and scribes were able to ensure the transmission of religious teachings and cultural heritage for generations to come.

Key Egyptian Symbols

When it comes to key symbols that were popularized in Egyptian culture, there are five that you need to be aware of. These five symbols are the first symbols that you will need to work with as a Kemetic practitioner, allowing you to remain in tune with Ma'at and your spirituality alike.

Ankh

The first symbol that is important to know is the Ankh. This symbol was used primarily to represent life, the immortal nature of life itself, and eternal existence as a whole. This symbol is one that you are probably personally familiar with, combining a looped cross that represents eternal life with a handle-like shape meant to symbolize both vitality and fertility.

Figure 3: Ankh

The main use of this symbolic key revolves around understanding our own existence beyond mortal boundaries. In essence, it represents life – not merely biological existence but spiritual continuity spanning birth, death, and rebirth.

When analyzing this fascinating icon further, one can see it embodies dualistic aspects representing male (the staff) and female (the oval), implying creation or fertility—the birthplace for new beginnings on both physical and spiritual planes.

Several artifacts from ancient Egypt depict deities holding Ankhs towards Pharaoh's nose - indicating 'giving breath of life' or 'breathing life into' someone after death. Such depictions emphasize beliefs about afterlife where one's Ka (spiritual double) continues living in another realm.

> *"The only difference between you and God is that you have forgotten you are divine."* ~ Marianne Williamson

This quote encapsulates how we often forget our cosmic origins amid worldly affairs - something which Kemetic practices aim to remind us of through symbols like the Ankh.

Renowned archaeologist Sir Flinders Petrie's studies highlight how Ankhs were extensively employed during religious rituals for sanctification purposes—echoing its role as a conduit between earthly realities and celestial energies.

Now let's discuss some practical examples where you could use Ankhs in your own spiritual practice:

1. Incorporating them within your meditation routine – Visualizing or holding an Ankh can serve as potent reminders about your eternal nature while meditating.

2. Using them for protection – Ancient Egyptians wore amulets featuring Ankhs believing they offered protection against negative forces.

3. Wearing them as jewelry – A simple yet effective way for constant reminders about your larger purpose beyond mere survival.

4. Adorning home spaces – Placing Ankhs at strategic locations around your house can help maintain positive energy flow while keeping you connected with ancestral wisdom.

In my personal practice, I engage the Ankh, both in physical form, and through visualization, for various energetic healings and other alchemical practices.

The Ankh is one of the most important symbols for Kemetic practitioners and it would be worth your time to create a deeper connection with it in your own personal practice.

Scarab

The next symbol to explore is the Scarab, which is actually a type of beetle. The scarab beetle was highly valued in ancient Egypt, due to its unique life cycle which the Egyptians associated with rebirth and regeneration. They observed how these beetles laid their eggs within dung balls that they rolled across the ground - an act they connected with Khepri, a solar deity who they believed rolled the sun across the sky each day. This association made the scarab a powerful symbol of transformation and renewal.

Figure 4: Scarab beetle rolling dung

In your journey through Kemetic spirituality, understanding this symbol will provide you much insight into their teachings on life, death and spiritual evolution. You'll discover how this simple insect became an emblem of one's ability to rise from difficulty and transform into something greater.

According to Smithsonian Institute's records, Ancient Egyptians created amulets shaped like Scarabs numbering over millions – signifying not just popularity but also the importance attached to this tiny creature across all different levels of society.

Scientists who have studied scarabs confirm what ancients Egyptians already knew: these beetles exhibit exceptional strength and perseverance. They can roll dung balls up to 50 times their weight—an astonishing feat that must have seemed magical to those watching thousands of years ago.

Consider for instance how author Jaycee Dugard, who was abducted as a child and held captive for 18 years, describes her encounter with a scarab during her captivity: "One morning I watched a small black bug struggling...I watched it push forward then fall back but never giving up...That little bug taught me determination." Such examples make it clear why this creature has been revered throughout history for its embodiment of resilience and determination.

Delving deeper into popular interpretations of this symbol might lead us towards answers about our own capacity for change. How often do we overlook or undervalue our strengths? How can we channel our inner 'scarab' when faced with obstacles?

Now let's discuss some ways you could incorporate lessons from 'Scarabeus sacer' (the sacred beetle) into your own life:

1. Start observing nature more closely; see patterns emerge mirroring themes found within Kemetics, such as renewal and regeneration, and interconnectedness of all beings.

2. Reflect upon transformations taking place within yourself – both subtle & dramatic ones.

3. Experiment using visual cues (like images, figurines or jewelry depicting Scarabs), anchoring them at places frequented most often so they serve as constant reminders and help to inspire transformational thoughts and actions.

Eye of Horus

Then, there is the Eye of Horus, which is also often called the Wadjet Eye (pronounced 'Wadjyet'), who was one of the earliest known Egyptian deities. She is often depicted as a cobra ready to strike - symbolizing her vigilant watchfulness against evil forces. This symbol is meant to represent protection, health, and royal power, and as such, many people will wear it in order to protect themselves. It embodies the healing and protective powers of the falcon-headed god Horus.

Figure 5: Eye of Horus (within an Ankh)

Adding more layers to its mysticism is its association with Thoth - god of wisdom – who restored Horus's eye after his epic battle with Set – god of chaos and confusion. Here arises an important metaphor for life's trials where we sometimes lose parts of ourselves only to find them healed or made whole again through wisdom and understanding.

I recommend incorporating this symbolism into your everyday life. One effective approach is through meditation, where you visualize the Eye of Horus. Additionally, consider wearing amulets or talismans featuring this symbol, a practice prevalent in ancient times for safeguarding against negative energies.

Eye of Ra

On the other hand, there is the eye of Ra, which is often called the Udjat or Wadjet eye. The Eye of Ra is closely related to the Eye of Horus and the two symbols are sometimes used interchangeably, especially in the context of protection and divine sight. The Eye of Ra, however, is a symbol associated with the sun god Ra, it represents the solar aspect of Ra, signifying protection, divine power, the sun's life-giving energy and its ability to illuminate darkness.

Figure 6: Eye of Ra

The Eye of Ra finds mention in various mythologies and texts from ancient Egypt. It is often depicted as a fierce entity personified by several goddesses such as Sekhmet, Wadjet, and Bastet who were known for their protective and destructive aspects. The eye played dual roles - it protected those who were loyal to Ra while also unleashing wrath upon his enemies. The Eye of Ra is not just an image; it's an embodiment of divine feminine energy with protective and destructive elements.

Historical records show instances where pharaohs used this symbol on their stelae or statues to ward off evil spirits or curses. Moreover, during certain festivals like 'Beautiful Feast of Wagy,' miniature eyes made from precious metals were buried with deceased Pharaohs to offer them protection in afterlife.

AWAKENING THE SACRED FLAME: A BEGINNER'S GUIDE... 135

Consider King Tutankhamun's golden death mask for instance; beautifully adorned with cobras (symbolizing Wadjet), and positioned above his forehead signifying protection offered by the Eye Of Ra.

Figure 7: King Tutankhamun's golden death mask

As with the Eye of Horus, you may choose to incorporate this symbol into your meditation practice, choosing whichever 'Eye' you resonate with most in terms of its spiritual and historical significance.

Djed Pillar

And the last symbol to note is the Djed Pillar. The Djed Pillar is a symbol of stability, endurance, and the resurrection of Osiris. It is associated with the backbone of Osiris and represents his enduring spirit.

The Djed Pillar, as can be seen in the image below, is depicted as a column with four horizontal lines at its top end. This image may seem simple but it is more than just lines on paper; each stroke signifies strength and resilience while the vertical line portrays continuity through time. Together they form an unshakeable support system - something we all need in our lives.

Figure 8: Djed Pillar (pictured on the left as the column with 4 lines at its top end)

Some ways you can incorporate the essence of the Djed Pillar into your life are as follows:

1. Acknowledge instability: Acceptance is always step one. Recognize moments when you're feeling unstable or uncertain.

2. Seek Balance: Find activities or practices that promote balance in your life such as meditation or yoga.

3. Cultivate Resilience: Build emotional strength to bounce back from setbacks.

4. Practice Continuity: Maintain consistency whether it be daily routines or long-term goals.

5. Embrace Regeneration: Allow yourself room to grow and evolve from experiences.

For those facing extreme adversities, where turmoil feels overwhelming, remember this - just like roots hold firmly even when storms rage above ground level; let your inner Djed strengthen you against life's trials.

Use of Art to Convey the Divine and Create a Sacred Atmosphere

Art was also immensely important to the ancient Egyptians. It was used to convey the divine and create a sacred atmosphere, among other things. For example, temples and tombs alike were adorned with intricate wall carvings, colorful paintings depicting gods, goddesses, religious rituals, and scenes from the afterlife. All of these artworks created a more sacred atmosphere within these environments.

Another artistic expression employed by the ancient Egyptians was the use of statues and reliefs to represent deities, Pharaohs, and other revered individuals. These statues acted as vessels for divine presence and veneration. Art in ancient Egypt overall conveyed the spiritual significance of rituals as well. For instance, art was used in offerings to the gods or as representative components of the journey of the deceased throughout the afterlife.

The intricate artistry and symbolic depictions in sacred spaces aimed to create a sense of awe, inspire devotion, and connect worshippers to the divine realm.

Color symbolism is also significant in Kemetic tradition. One of the most notable instances of color symbolism in Kemetic tradition is the use of gold, a shimmering embodiment of the divine itself. The radiant hue of gold transcends mere material richness; it encapsulates the essence of the gods and goddesses who watched over the land of Egypt. The gleaming gold of temples and artifacts wasn't just a reflection of earthly wealth; it was a testament to the spiritual opulence that resided within the heart of the civilization. When incorporating gold into artworks, rituals, or spaces, one not only adorns the physical but also invokes the presence of the divine, creating a space where the sacred and the mundane converge.

Likewise, green emerges as a vibrant messenger of nature's cycles—fertility and rebirth. Just as the lush banks of the Nile River nourished the land and brought life anew, the color green serves as a reminder of the constant cycle of creation and renewal. When woven into sacred arts, green breathes vitality into the creative process and invites the energies of growth and transformation. Its presence resonates with the heartbeat of the earth and aligns the practitioner with the rhythms of the natural world.

Here are some examples of other colors used in Kemetic artwork:

- **Yellow:** Yellow was linked to the sun and often depicted in the color of the sun disc. Both gold and yellow were used to depict the radiance and cosmic energy of the divine.

- **Blue:** Blue represented water and the heavens. It was associated with the sky, the Nile River, and creation. Blue was often used to represent the primeval waters from which all life emerged, signifying both the source of life and the cosmic expanse.

- **Red:** Red symbolized vitality, life force, and protection. It was often associated with the god Set, who had a dual nature of chaos and protection. Red also had protective qualities and was used in amulets and charms.

- **White:** White represented purity, innocence, and cleanliness. It was associated with light and was often used in religious contexts to depict divine beings and sacred offerings.

- **Black:** Black was connected to death, the unknown, and the mysteries of the afterlife. It was also symbolic of fertility and regeneration, as the rich black soil of the Nile Delta allowed for abundant agricultural growth.

- **Brown:** Brown was used to depict the earth and the fertile soil along the banks of the Nile. It represented stability, grounding, and the physical world.

Understanding the nuances of color symbolism in Kemetic tradition allows practitioners to harness the power of hues intentionally. By strategically infusing gold and green into artworks, rituals, and spaces, one can amplify the resonance of the divine and the fertile energies of rebirth. Just as the ancient Egyptians wove these colors into their daily lives, we, too, can draw upon their wisdom to evoke spiritual depth, connect with the gods, and align with the rhythms of creation. In this artful dance of colors, the vibrancy of Kemetic spirituality comes to life, bridging the past and the present in a tapestry of meaning and significance.

Importance of Music and Dance in Religious Ceremonies

Music and dance also played an integral role in religious ceremonies within ancient Egyptian culture. Music and dance were used within religious ceremonies as a vehicle for spiritual expression, as well as a way to connect with the divine. Musicians in ancient Egypt played various instruments, including harps, flutes, drums, and sistra. Enhancing the sacred atmosphere of a ritual as well as invoking the presence of the gods, was of the essence to ancient Egyptians, meaning that music was crucial.

Dances were important as well. Oftentimes, dances were performed by priests and/or temple attendants, and these dances were considered to be sacred rituals due to the belief that they embodied cosmic rhythms and myths.

Ancient Egyptians believed every action had a rhythm. They regarded dance and music as an embodiment of cosmic harmony — the ebb and flow of the universe reflected in their bodies' movements. For example, some dances symbolize the cycles of creation and rebirth. This notion was deeply integrated into their worship practices, leading to a unique blend of spirituality interwoven with melody and grace.

Science has shown us that frequencies can influence our state of consciousness — from high-energy beats inciting excitement to slow-paced melodies inducing relaxation or meditation. The Ancient Egyptians leveraged this knowledge during religious rites, utilizing specific sonic patterns to induce altered states necessary for spiritual connection.

Imagine yourself standing on the banks of the River Nile thousands of years ago; you hear the soft strums of lyres echoing through temple halls while priestesses perform sacred dances under moonlit skies. These harmonious rituals were not merely aesthetic spectacles but integral parts of spiritual practices aimed at appeasing deities and evoking divine energy.

The importance these art forms hold is evident when we consider ancient artifacts like wall carvings depicting priests playing sistrums or dancers moving ecstatically during festivals honoring gods like Hathor — often associated with music, dance, joy, love, motherhood and feminine beauty.

Both music and dance were believed to be forms of communication with the gods, heightening spiritual experiences and facilitating communion with the divine.

If your interest in Kemetic spirituality deepens beyond casual curiosity into genuine practice remember this advice - immerse yourself completely in these arts without reservation or inhibition; let go off preconceived notions about dance being merely physical movement or music just being sounds strung together. Only then can you truly appreciate their profound significance within this ancient tradition.

By exploring the symbolism, and sacred arts of ancient Egypt, individuals can deepen their understanding of Kemetic spirituality, gain insights into ancient Egyptian culture and beliefs, and apply these teachings to their own spiritual journeys.

BONUS: Decoding the Language of Dreams

> *"All men whilst they are awake are in one common world: but each of them, when he is asleep, is in a world of his own."*
> —Plutarch

Imagine the last time you woke up from a dream, your heart pounding with adrenaline, your mind alive with vibrant images. This is where we start our journey into the realm of Kemetic spirituality and dream interpretation.

Kemetic spirituality views dreams as more than mere flights of fancy. It regards them as divine messages from the spiritual realm. This philosophy suggests that our dreams are a crucial intersection between us and the divine, a cryptic language waiting to be decoded.

When you drift off to sleep, your conscious mind takes a hiatus, allowing your subconscious mind to commune with the divine. Each dream you experience is a spiritual message designed specifically for you. For instance, dreaming about water might symbolize purification or transformation in your life.

This perspective isn't merely philosophical; it's supported by modern psychology. Carl Jung, a pioneer in dream analysis, also believed that dreams provide valuable insights into our subconscious minds. He proposed that symbols in dreams—like water—represent universal archetypes that can be interpreted to understand our inner world.

Kemetic dream interpretation plays a pivotal role in personal growth and self-improvement. By interpreting and understanding your dreams, you gain insights into your fears, desires, and potential. For example, if you often dream about failing a test or an examination, it might indicate underlying anxieties about not meeting expectations. A recurring nightmare about being chased could signal that you're avoiding something in your waking life.

These interpretations aren't arbitrary; they're based on centuries-old wisdom from ancient Egypt. The Egyptians believed that dreams were messages from the gods that could foretell future events or reveal hidden truths about oneself. Today's psychologists also think that recurring themes in dreams often reflect unresolved issues or deep-seated fears in our waking lives.

Dreams have been one of the primary mediums through which I've received messages from the divine. Although I never consciously sought out these experiences, they seem to be the preferred method of communication with me for the divine.

In my dreams, I've heard crystal-clear messages that were communicated verbally to me. Some of my other dreams have been more abstract, often featuring an animal—usually a snake—that leaves me with a sense of its significance upon waking. It was through these serpentine dreams that the divine mother goddess Isis (*Aset*) beckoned me forth.

Similarly, warnings about future events in my life have come through such dreams involving snakes. And other impactful dreams leading me towards ancient Egyptian teachings, include one where I saw myself floating down the Nile—a location I later visited during my pilgrimage to Egypt.

The Eye of Ra is another potent symbol that has emerged in my dreams, further solidifying my connection with ancient Egypt. Interpreting these mystical and beautiful dream experiences has been one of the most fascinating aspects on this spiritual journey—one which I encourage others to pay attention to.

***

The beauty of Kemetic spirituality and dream interpretation is its accessibility. You don't need any special tools or rituals. All you need is an open mind and a willingness to listen to the divine messages woven into your dreams.

So, think back to that dream you woke up from, heart pounding and mind buzzing—it was more than just a dream. It was a divine message, a spiritual roadmap guiding you through your path. Embracing Kemetic spirituality and dream interpretation is like learning a new language, one that connects you to the divine and enriches your daily life in ways you could never have imagined.

Dream Interpretation in Ancient Egypt

The concept of dream interpretation, often associated with "New Age" thinking, is not a modern invention. It has roots that extend thousands of years back to the time of the ancient Egyptians. In the eyes of the ancient Egyptians, dreams were not mere figments of the subconscious mind, but direct channels for divine guidance and insight. They believed that the gods communicated with them through dreams, providing wisdom and forewarnings about the future.

This belief was so deeply ingrained in their culture that it influenced various aspects of their lives. Dreams were held in such high regard that they had the potential to guide decisions on matters ranging from health to politics and even warfare. Understanding your dreams was thus an integral part of ancient Egyptian culture.

The Dream Book

To help decipher these divine messages, the ancient Egyptians developed a complex system of dream interpretation documented in texts like the "Dream Book" or "Book of Dreams." This papyrus document, written in hieratic script—a simplified version of hieroglyphics—dates back to the early reign of Ramesses II (1279-1213 B.C.).

Each page begins with a vertical column translating to 'If a man sees himself in a dream,' followed by horizontal lines describing different dreams and their interpretations. For instance, 'If a man sees himself in a dream looking out of a window, good; it means the hearing of his cry.' The book categorizes dreams into 'good' or 'bad,' with bad ones notably written in red—the color associated with bad omens.

The 'Dream Book' records around 108 dreams encompassing 78 activities and emotions, providing a fascinating glimpse into the psyche of the ancient Egyptians. The most common themes revolved around sight or seeing, followed by eating and drinking. Other activities included receiving and copulating.

Some common dream images and their meanings, as per ancient Egyptian dream interpretation, include:

- Looking out of a window: Considered good; it means the hearing of one's cry.

- Breaking stones: Notably categorized as a good dream, the interpretation isn't specified.

- Losing teeth: A warning of impending chaos or disorder.

Deity Influence on Dreams

In ancient Egypt, it was believed that the deities played a pivotal role in shaping dreams. Each god or goddess was linked to specific facets of life, with individuals seeking their guidance and protection across various circumstances—dreams included. Some ways these divine beings were perceived to sway dream scenarios include:

Bes, the Household Guardian: Bes was a dwarf deity celebrated for his protective qualities over households. To stave off nightmares and safeguard their homes, people would call upon Bes. His presence symbolized comfort and security, making him a popular figure in dream-related rituals.

Serket, the Goddess of Healing: Also known as Selcis, Serket was revered for her healing powers and protective nature. It was thought that she could send dreams as a therapeutic method for those who were ill. Anyone in search of healing may have sought guidance or insights from Serket through their dreams.

Bastet, Protector of Homes: Dreams featuring large cats—symbolic representations of Bastet—were seen as favorable omens. As the goddess associated with home safety and protection, such visions indicated promising prospects for harvests, homes, and families alike; they signified positive energies at work.

Seeking the assistance and favor of specific deities in dreams was part of a broader spiritual practice aimed at aligning oneself with divine guidance and protection. The choice of deity often depended on the nature of the dream and the desired outcome, reflecting the deep intertwining of religious beliefs and daily life in ancient Egyptian society.

Dream Interpreters

In ancient Egypt, the quest for understanding dreams led individuals to seek the expertise of specialists, who were often priests or professional dream interpreters. An ancient tablet inscription boldly declared, 'I interpret dreams, having the gods' mandate to do so.' This not only emphasized the presence of a divine mandate, but also endowed these specialists with a perceived divine authority in their work.

This practice of dream interpretation held profound cultural significance, intricately woven into the fabric of Egyptian society. It not only influenced decision-making, but also guided actions and provided insights into both personal and communal matters. The involvement of specialists added a distinct layer of religious authority, underscoring the sacred nature of the interpretation process.

Dreams in ancient Egypt were like intricate tapestries woven with symbols—often carrying messages straight from the divine realm. Interpreters, trained in unraveling this symbolism, connected the dreamer's experiences with broader spiritual and cosmic themes.

Beyond their roles as skilled interpreters, these specialists were regarded as mediators between the earthly and divine realms. Far from being mere intellectual analyses, their interpretations served as conduits for communication between gods and people—providing guidance and foresight.

The insights derived from dream interpretation held the power to influence pivotal decisions at both personal and societal levels. As touched on previously, leaders, including pharaohs, sought the counsel of dream interpreters before making consequential choices related to governance, warfare, and other critical matters. The interwoven network of dream interpretation by specialists under divine guidance underscores how profoundly dreams influenced both cultural norms and spiritual beliefs in ancient Egypt.

Dream Incubation

Dream incubation, a notable practice in ancient Egypt, was deeply rooted in the culture because of its perceived ability to facilitate divine communication. Dream temples—sacred spaces dedicated to specific gods—were frequented by individuals seeking guidance or solutions through their dreams. The uniqueness of dream temples lay in their accessibility to people from all walks of life. Regardless of social status, anyone could seek divine counsel within these halls. This openness reflected a belief that every person had the potential for spiritual connection via their dreams.

Here is how the dream incubation would unfold:

Preparation and Purification

Prior to entering the temple, individuals participated in purification rituals. These could encompass actions such as cleansing baths, abstaining from specific foods or even fasting. The aim was to attain both physical and spiritual purity in preparation for an elevated spiritual experience.

Selection of Deity

Visitors selected a particular deity who they believed could provide the guidance or solution they were seeking. Each god or goddess was thought to possess unique powers and spheres of influence. The person would show their faith in their chosen deity through prayers and invocations.

Rituals and Offerings

Once inside the temple, rituals and offerings were presented to the chosen deity. These ceremonies aimed at invoking the presence of the selected god or goddess; with rhythmic chants, incense burning, and atmospheric temple surroundings all contributing towards creating a sacred space.

Cultivating Dreams in Sacred Space

After completing preparatory rituals, individuals spent the night within the confines of the temple—often in specially designated areas—as sleeping within this sacred space was deemed crucial for the dream incubation process. The expectation being that during sleep, the chosen deity would talk via dreams.

Dream Interpretation

Upon awakening, dreamers shared their dreams with priests or appointed interpreters present within the temple confines. Interpreting these dreams formed a significant part of this process, since messages received were considered as divine guidance for life's path.

Reflection & Action

Post-dream interpretation, dreamers reflected on insights gleaned from these divine messages. Often times, taking specific actions based on received guidance. Whether seeking advice on personal issues, health concerns or decisions, dreamers placed their trust in the belief that these dreams had imparted valuable information.

Overall, dream incubation in ancient Egypt represented a holistic approach to spirituality, where individuals actively invited divine intervention through an accessible and sacred practice. The open-door policy of these temples, coupled with the emphasis on personal spiritual readiness, underlined the belief that anyone—irrespective of societal standing—could engage directly with the divine via dreams.

***

The ancient Egyptians' approach to dream interpretation reveals their deep reverence for dreams as divine messages and their sophisticated understanding of the subconscious mind. Their practices continue to intrigue us today, offering a unique perspective on the human psyche and our timeless quest for meaning in our dreams.

What does all this mean for you? It means that you have access to a powerful tool used by one of history's most advanced civilizations—right in your sleep. By learning how to interpret your dreams, you can gain insights about your life and spiritual path.

Dream Interpretation For The Kemetic Practitioner

To connect with the Netjeru in your own dreams, consider the following:

1. Keep a dream journal beside your bed.

2. Before sleep, meditate on the query in your mind and the specific god/goddess you wish to commune with. Ask them to communicate with you in your sleep in a way that you can understand and will remember. This may be something like *"God/Goddess [name of deity], please provide guidance to me on [topic] through my dreams tonight. Please communicate it to me in a way that I will understand and that I will remember."*

3. As soon as you wake from a dream, note down everything you remember—every detail matters.

4. Pay particular attention to any recurring themes or symbols.

5. Note the emotional tone of the dream. Emotions can provide insights into the dream's significance. Kemetic spirituality often emphasizes the connection between emotions and spiritual experiences.

6. Use resources on Kemetic symbolism to understand the meanings of specific symbols.

7. Consider what each symbol might represent in relation to Kemetic deities or principles.

8. Reflect on how this could be relevant to your query, your current

life situation, or spiritual journey. Dreams often reflect aspects of our waking life, and interpreting them in the context of your present situation can provide valuable insights.

9. Trust your intuition and inner guidance. Sometimes, the meaning of a dream becomes clearer through a deep, personal understanding.

10. During meditation, revisit your dreams. Allow the symbolism to unfold and explore how it aligns with your spiritual journey.

Establishing communication with the Netjeru through dreams, like any other skill, needs patience and consistent practice. And as I can personally attest, sometimes these dreams occur spontaneously without any conscious intent.

In addition, while all dreams have the potential to be meaningful—reflecting our subconscious minds or spiritual experiences—not all of them are significant in terms of divine communication; indeed, most aren't. The ones that do hold such significance—what I refer to as 'power dreams'—often conclude at the moment of awakening for easier recall. They carry an inherent sense of importance and leave you with the distinct impression that they bear a message.

Patience is key here; trust that the guidance you seek will be communicated and received at just the right time.

Common Symbolism For Kemetic Dream Interpretation

Unraveling the symbolism in Kemetic dream interpretation could fill an entire book. Nevertheless, let's looks at some of the key symbols and their potential meanings here:

Ankh

☥

Symbolism: Life, immortality, eternal existence, fertility.

Interpretation: Dreaming of an Ankh may signify a connection with the eternal aspects of life or a message about the continuity of the soul beyond physical existence. It may also represent divine union, or that you are divinely protected.

Deities: Associated with various deities, including Osiris and Isis.

Djed Pillar

Symbolism: Stability, endurance, strength.

Interpretation: Represents spiritual fortitude, resilience.

Deities: Linked to Osiris, god of the Underworld and death, and Ptah, god of creation.

Eye of Horus

Symbolism: Protection, healing, and divine insight.

Interpretation: Dreaming of the Eye of Horus may indicate that you are under the watchful protection of divine forces, or it could symbolize a need for healing and gaining spiritual insight. Sacrifice is also a common connotation.

Deities: Associated with the sky god Horus.

BONUS: Decoding the Language of Dreams (SPLIT)

Eye of Ra

Symbolism: Sun, solar power, divine protection.

Interpretation: Dreaming of the Eye of Ra may signify divine protection, insight, and the watchful gaze of the gods over your life.

Deities: Equated with the sun god Ra.

Falcon

Symbolism: Protection, vision, and divine guidance.

Interpretation: Seeing a falcon in a dream may indicate a protective presence watching over you, heightened spiritual insight, or guidance in a specific aspect of your life.

Deities: Associated with the sky god Horus.

Feather of Ma'at

Symbolism: Truth, justice, cosmic balance.

Interpretation: Seeing the feather of Ma'at in a dream may suggest the importance of living in alignment with truth and ethical principles in your waking life.

Deities: Associated with the goddess Ma'at.

Hieroglyphs

Symbolism: Sacred script, divine communication.

Interpretation: Dreaming of hieroglyphs may suggest the need to decipher hidden messages in your life, or a call to explore ancient wisdom for guidance.

Deities: No specific deity association.

Lotus Flower

Symbolism: Purity, rebirth, and spiritual enlightenment.

Interpretation: Dreaming of a lotus flower could signify a period of personal growth, new beginnings, spiritual awakening or purification, or the blossoming of inner wisdom.

Deities: Linked to creation myths and the goddess Isis.

Mummification

Symbolism: Death and the afterlife, preservation, and the journey to the eternal realm.

Interpretation: Dreaming of mummification may suggest a need for inner preservation, preparing for a significant transition, or exploring the mysteries of life and death on a spiritual level.

Deities: Linked to Osiris, god of the afterlife.

Obelisk

Symbolism: Connection between Earth and divine, stability.

Interpretation: Dreaming of an obelisk may signify a desire for spiritual elevation, the need for spiritual grounding, a connection with higher realms, or the pursuit of divine wisdom.

Deities: No specific deity association.

Ouroboros

Symbolism: Rebirth, a new beginning, and an eternal cycle.

Interpretation: In a dream, the Ouroboros may indicate a period of personal transformation and spiritual growth. It suggests that you are in a phase of renewal, shedding old habits or beliefs and embracing new beginnings.

Deities: No specific deity association.

Papyrus or Reed

Symbolism: Growth, abundance, and resilience.

Interpretation: Dreaming of papyrus or reeds may suggest a period of growth, a call to be resilient in the face of challenges, or the potential for abundant opportunities in your life.

Deities: No specific deity association.

Pyramids

Symbolism: Spiritual ascension and growth, the afterlife.

Interpretation: Dreaming of pyramids might suggest that you are on a spiritual journey, seeking higher knowledge, or that you are aligning yourself with cosmic energies.

Deities: Associated with various cosmic deities.

Scarab Beetle

Symbolism: Regeneration, transformation, protection.

Interpretation: Encountering a Scarab in a dream may suggest a period of transformation or renewal in your life, and it may also signify protection on your spiritual journey.

Deities: Linked to the sun god Ra.

Serpent

Symbolism: Transformation, protection, cycles of life, and the duality of creation and destruction.

Interpretation: Dreaming of a serpent may signify a transformative process in your life, shedding old habits or beliefs. It could also indicate protection on your spiritual journey or the need to navigate dualities with wisdom and balance.

Deities: Associated with various serpent deities, including Wadjet and Apep.

Sistrum

Symbolism: The Sistrum is a musical instrument symbolizing joy, music, and divine feminine energy.

Interpretation: Seeing or hearing a Sistrum in a dream may indicate a call to embrace joy, creativity, or a deeper connection with the feminine aspects of spirituality.

Deities: Often used in worship rituals, associated with goddess Hathor.

Sun Disk

Symbolism: Solar power, light, energy, and life force.

Interpretation: Dreaming of a sun disk may suggest a period of enlightenment, renewed energy, or a connection with the life force that empowers your spiritual path.

Deities: Associated with the sun god Ra.

Temple

Symbolism: Sacred spaces for worship, reflection, and communion with the divine.

Interpretation: Dreaming of a temple may signify a need for spiritual retreat, a quest for inner reflection, or a desire for a deeper connection with the divine.

Deities: Associated with various temple deities.

***

While I have provided here some common meanings and potential interpretations, it's crucial to remember that interpreting dreams is subjective, and personal associations with symbols can differ greatly. These interpretations draw inspiration from Kemetic spirituality's symbolism and can act as launching pads for deciphering potential messages within your dreams.

As time goes on and with practice, you'll cultivate an intuitive understanding of your own dream symbols. So tonight, as you surrender yourself to sleep, bear in mind—there could be a divine message waiting for you in your dreams.

***

In the realm of Kemetic Spirituality, where the tangible and the ethereal converge, dream interpretation becomes a sacred art, a journey into the mysteries of the soul. As we navigate the landscape of our dreams, we walk hand in hand with the divine, unraveling the symbolic tapestry woven by the gods. Each dream is a chapter in the cosmic story of our spiritual existence. They are dialogues between mortal and divine, scripted in the language of symbols.

May your nights be filled with dreams that illuminate the path of your spiritual journey, and may the whispers of the gods guide you to the deepest recesses of your soul, revealing the profound truths that shape your waking reality. In the dance between sleep and wakefulness, may you find the wisdom to navigate the labyrinth of your spiritual path with grace and purpose.

Conclusion

"There are many paths but only one journey." ~ Naomi Judd

Embarking upon the journey of Kemetic spirituality allows you to embrace ancient wisdom and connect with the profound teachings offered by Ma'at, the Netjeru, and the symbolism spearheaded by ancient Egypt. By being diligent in cultivating devotion, exploring the sacred texts of Egypt, honoring ancestors, and engaging with various rituals and practices, you have the ability to find inner peace, personal growth, and develop a profound connection with the universe. This path offers those who follow it the ability to align with universal spiritual principles, timeless guidance for ethical living, and transformative experiences that apply to modern interpretations of Kemetic spirituality. You can ignite your inner flame and awaken your divine potential by embracing the rich tapestry of Kemetic spirituality.

In all, Kemetic spirituality offers a journey to a deeper connection with oneself and the world around them, alongside the principles of Ma'at and their offering of a guiding light for ethical living, balance, justice, compassion, wisdom, and more. Now, you understand these central principles, including the value of cultivating relationships with the deities of ancient Egypt, venerating ancestors for a profound sense of connection and the ability to honor ancient wisdom and more. You are in tune with sacred texts that can offer insights, as well as the symbols, art, and more that help to convey spiritual concepts.

Integrating ancient Kemetic wisdom into modern interpretations can offer many meaningful insights and practices for contemporary spiritual speakers. If you feel the call of devotion, if it is something that resonates with you, then I encourage you to follow it. Use the tools you have learned here to foster a new life—one where your spirituality can truly root itself and flourish.

And remember, while the spiritual journey is one that is shared by many, there are many paths on that journey, and there is no rush, as there is no end goal. The spiritual journey is forever unfolding, it is the journey of life. Echoing the wisdom of Joseph Campbell; *"If you can see your path laid out in front of you step by step, you know it's not your path. Your own path you make with every step you take. That's why it's your path."* So come to know thyself, connect with your own inner wisdom, trust in your guidance, and from there you will find the richness in your unique journey.

***

If you've found the resources within this book to be useful, please consider leaving a review to allow those interested in Kemeticism to find this valuable resource. At the end of the day, remember that Kemetic spirituality is a lifelong process wherein we reap benefits that are reciprocated between us and the Netjeru. By embodying Ma'at and continuing on your journey, you have what it takes to become a skillful Kemetic practitioner.

If you would like to leave a review, all you have to do is scan the QR code to be taken to the books review page.

Thanks for your support!

FREE ENERGY HEALING MEDITATION

Are you ready to recalibrate your energy with the healing touch of goddess Isis?

As we journey through life there are many things that contribute to stagnant or blocked energy in our field. These blockages can lead us feeling depleted, disconnected, and disenchanted with life.

The Energy Healing Meditation, channeled by Katherine through her connection with goddess Isis, is a transformative journey into the sacred chambers of Isis's Philae temple.

This guided meditation serves as a tool for spiritual healing, facilitating a deep connection with the divine feminine energy embodied by Isis. Through the recalibration process, you may experience a realignment of your energy centers, fostering a sense of balance, clarity, and heightened spiritual awareness.

The meditation taps into the ancient wisdom encoded in the Philae Temple's sacred vibrations, infusing the energy recalibration with the potent healing frequencies associated with goddess Isis. Participants often report a sense of release from stagnant energies, emotional blockages, and even physical tension.

The energies harnessed here contribute to a spiritual journey that transcends time, providing contemporary seekers with a bridge to the sacred practices of ancient Kemetic spirituality.

Download your FREE Energy Healing Meditation by scanning the QR code below:

Is it hard for you to manifest your desires into reality?

Did you know that the ancient Egyptians hold the secret mystery keys to successful manifestation?

For 3,000 years these 3 manifestation keys have stood the test of time.

And you can use them now to manifest the right way.

Scan the QR code below to download the 3 manifesting keys from Ancient Egypt for FREE:

Glossary

Altar: A sacred space or shrine where offerings, prayers, and rituals are performed to honor deities or spirits.

Ancestral Veneration: A practice of honoring and showing respect to one's ancestors and the ancestors of the land, seeking their guidance and protection.

Ankh: The Ankh symbolizes life, immortality, and eternal existence. It combines a looped cross, representing eternal life, with a handle-like shape symbolizing vitality and fertility.

Anubis: An ancient Egyptian deity associated with mummification, funerals, and the afterlife. Often depicted as a jackal-headed figure.

Bastet: An ancient Egyptian goddess of home, fertility, and protection, usually represented as a lioness or a woman with a lioness head.

Beautiful Feast of Wagy: This occasion held a link to the funerary ceremonies of ancient Egypt. Individuals in non-religious contexts also observed it both within the important temples of Egypt and beyond the confines of official religious gatherings.

Book of the Dead: A collection of ancient Egyptian religious texts that provided guidance for the deceased's journey through the afterlife.

Coffin Text: Ancient Egyptian funerary spells and religious teachings, primarily inscribed on coffins and sarcophagi intended to guide and protect the deceased in their journey through the afterlife. These texts were not exclusively reserved for pharaohs but could be inscribed on the coffins of high-ranking officials and individuals.

Deity: In the context of spirituality, a deity refers to a divine or supernatural being, often worshipped and revered for its powers and influence over specific aspects of life or the cosmos.

Djed Pillar: The Djed Pillar symbolizes stability, endurance, and the resurrection of Osiris. It is associated with the backbone of Osiris and represents his enduring spirit.

Eye of Horus: The Eye of Horus represents protection, health, and royal power. It embodies the healing and protective powers of the falcon-headed god Horus.

Eye of Ra: The Eye of Ra represents the solar aspect of Ra, signifying protection, divine power, and the sun's life-giving energy.

Funerary Text: A collection of ancient Egyptian religious and magical writings intended for use in funerary practices. These texts were crucial for guiding the deceased through the afterlife and ensuring a successful transition.

Hathor: A revered goddess with associations to music, dance, love, motherhood, and joy, often depicted as a cow-headed deity.

Heb: Ancient Egyptian festivals celebrated as part of religious and cultural traditions.

Heka: The ancient Egyptian term for magic or divine power, often associated with the spoken word or rituals performed by priests.

Horus: A significant deity symbolizing kingship, protection, and the divine falcon, often depicted as a falcon-headed god or as a human pharaoh with a falcon's crown.

Isis: An ancient Egyptian goddess of motherhood, magic, and wisdom, known as the mother and protector of the pharaoh.

Ma'at: The concept of order, balance, and truth in ancient Egyptian belief. Ma'at was both a goddess and a cosmic principle.

Medu Neter: The ancient Egyptian writing system, now known as hieroglyphs, denoted as "divine words", "divine speech" or "divine language." These sacred symbols were employed for religious, monumental, and administrative inscriptions.

Netjeru: The plural term for deities in ancient Egyptian religion, also known as gods and goddesses.

Osiris: An ancient Egyptian god of the afterlife and resurrection, often depicted as a mummified pharaoh.

Pantheon: A group or collection of deities or gods and goddesses within a particular religious tradition.

Pharaoh: The title used for the rulers of ancient Egypt who were believed to have divine authority as intermediaries between the gods and the people.

Polytheistic: The belief in or worship of multiple gods and goddesses, as opposed to monotheism, which believes in one god.

Psychopomp: Derived from the Greek words "psyche", meaning soul, and "pompos", meaning guide or conductor, a psychopomp is a spiritual being, deity, or guide that is believed to escort the souls of the deceased to the afterlife.

Pyramid Texts: Ancient Egyptian religious texts inscribed on the walls of pyramids, containing spells and rituals for the pharaoh's journey to the afterlife.

Ra: The ancient Egyptian sun god, one of the most important deities in the pantheon, often depicted with a falcon head and a solar disk.

Reconstruction: A modern religious approach that seeks to revive and reconstruct ancient religious practices, rituals, and beliefs based on historical evidence.

Sacred Text: Texts that hold religious significance and are revered as divine or authoritative within a religious tradition.

Scarab: The Scarab beetle symbolizes regeneration and rebirth. Egyptians associated it with the sun and believed it rolled the sun across the sky like the Scarab beetle rolling a ball of dung.

Sekhmet: Sekhmet: The lioness-headed goddess associated with war, healing, and the destructive forces of the sun, embodying both protective and fierce aspects.

Stelae: A stele (stelae in plural form) is a tall and relatively narrow stone or wooden slab that was commonly erected as a monument in the ancient world. These structures typically feature text, decorations, or a combination of both on their surfaces.

Thoth: An ancient Egyptian deity associated with wisdom, writing, and magic, often depicted as an ibis-headed or baboon-headed figure.

Wadjet: A protective goddess often depicted as a cobra and associated with the Eye of Ra, symbolizing healing, protection, and the watchful power of the sun.

Further Reading

This book provides an introduction to Kemetic spirituality, offering a concise overview of the topics to provide beginners with an accessible entry into its practices. For a deeper exploration, you may consider the recommended reading materials provided below. It's important to note that the inclusion of a book on this list does not imply complete agreement with every aspect of its content; our recommended readings are diverse and aim to offer varying perspectives.

Theology and Philosophy

Conceptions of God in Ancient Egypt: The One and the Many, *by Erik Hornung*

Daily Life of the Egyptian Gods, *by Christine Favard-Meeks and Dimitri Meeks*

Egyptian Mythology: A Guide to the Gods, Goddesses, and Traditions of Ancient Egypt, *by Geraldine Pinch*

Complete Gods and Goddesses of Ancient Egypt, *by Richard H. Wilkinson*

Reading Egyptian Art: A Hieroglyphic Guide to Ancient Egyptian Painting and Sculpture, *by Richard H. Wilkinson*

Literature

Echoes of Egyptian Voices: An Anthology of Ancient Egyptian Poetry, *by John L. Foster*

Ancient Egyptian Literature, *by Miriam Lichtheim*

Voices from Ancient Egypt: An Anthology of Middle Kingdom Writings, *by Richard B. Parkinson*

History and Society

Chronicle of the Pharaohs: The Reign-By-Reign Record of the Rulers and Dynasties of Ancient Egypt, *by Peter Clayton*

The Calendars of Ancient Egypt, *by R.A. Parker*

Ancient Lives: Daily Life in Egypt of the Pharaohs, *by John Romer*

Funerary Texts

The Egyptian Book of the Dead: The Book of Going Forth by Day: The Papyrus of Ani, *by Dr. Raymond Faulkner (Translator), Ogden Goelet (Translator), Carol Andrews (Preface), J. Daniel Gunther (Introduction), James Wasserman (Foreword)*

The Ancient Egyptian Pyramid Texts, *by R. O. Faulkner*

The Ancient Egyptian Coffin Texts, *by R. O. Faulkner*

The Pyramid Texts of Unas, *by A. Piankoff*

References

6 Ways to Cleanse a Room and Purify Your Space. (n.d.). Konmari.com. Retrieved July 15, 2023, from https://konmari.com/home-purification/#:~:text =While%20most%20commonly%20burned%20for

Ancient Egyptian Literature: Wisdom Texts - Literature & Hieroglyphs - Per-Ankh: Ancient Egypt. (n.d.). Www.per-Ankh.co.uk . http://www.perankh.co.uk/monuments_of_egypt/literature_and_hierogly phs/ancient_egyptian_literature_wisdom_texts.asp

Budgell, C. A. (2018, December 1). *How to Create an Altar for Your Own Unique Practice*. Wanderlust. https://wanderlust.com/journal/how-to-create-an-altar-for-your-own-unique -practice/#:~:text=Wanderlust%20teacher%20Sally%20Sherman%20keeps

Egypt: Perchance to Dream: Dreams and Their Meaning in Ancient Egypt. (Stratos, A., 2013). Tour Egypt. http://www.touregypt.net/featurestories/dr eam.htm

Gods. (2017, December 3). Kemet Expert. https://kemetexpert.com/category /gods/

Heka | Kemet.org. (n.d.). Www.kemet.org. Retrieved July 15, 2023, from http s://www.kemet.org/taxonomy/term/85

How to Use a Dowsing Pendulum For Divination – Beginner's Guide. (2022, Jan 13). Loner Wolf. https://lonerwolf.com/dowsing-pendulum/

San-Aset. (2020, July 13). *The Seven Principles of Ma'at*. Iseum Sanctuary. https://iseumsanctuary.com/2020/07/12/the-seven-principles-of-maat/

Spiritual Cleansing: 14 Rituals to Detox Your Soul. (2023, January 5). Yoga Basics. https://www.yogabasics.com/connect/yoga-blog/spiritual-cleansing/

The Editors of Encyclopedia Britannica. (2014). Scarab | Egyptian symbol. In *Encyclopædia Britannica*. https://www.britannica.com/topic/scarab

Warren, K. (n.d.). *Book of the Dead: A Guidebook to the Afterlife*. ARCE. https://arce.org/resource/book-dead-guidebook-afterlife/

Image References

aeramedia. (n.d.). *Egypt Eye Horus* [Image]. Pixabay. https://pixabay.com/illustrations/egypt-eye-horus-hieroglyphics-5973540/

AlexPee07. (n.d.). *Hieroglyphs, Pharaohs, Egypt image* [Image]. Pixabay. https://pixabay.com/photos/hieroglyphs-pharaohs-egypt-luxor-429863/

Barthwo. (n.d.). *Ankh, Egypt, Hieroglyphs image* [Image]. Pixabay. https://pixabay.com/photos/ankh-egypt-hieroglyphs-symbols-105769/

ha11ok. (n.d.). *Ank, Cross, Spiritual* [Image]. Pixabay. https://pixabay.com/photos/ank-cross-spiritual-egypt-egyptian-1215064/

Topi_Pigula. (n.d.). *Scarab, Beetle, God image* [Image]. Pixabay. https://pixabay.com/photos/scarab-beetle-god-shit-italy-2490586/

LorettaLynn. (n.d.). *Stone relief, Egypt, Ancient image* [Image]. Pixabay. https://pixabay.com/photos/stone-relief-egypt-ancient-temple-590803/

Sriom. (n.d.). *Tutankhamun, Pharaoh, Gold mask image* [Image]. Pixabay. https://pixabay.com/photos/tutankhamun-pharaoh-gold-mask-king-509752/

DEZALB. (n.d.). *Egypt, Kom-ombo, Temple image* [Image]. Pixabay. https://pixabay.com/photos/egypt-kom-ombo-temple-engraving-3382563/

Clker-Free-Vector-Images. (n.d.). *Horus God Egypt royalty-free vector graphic* [Image]. Pixabay. https://pixabay.com/vectors/horus-god-egypt-religion-mythology-33962/

Clker-Free-Vector-Images. (n.d.). *Egypt Hieroglyph Goddess* [Image]. Pixabay. https://pixabay.com/vectors/egypt-hieroglyph-goddess-isis-33967/

Clker-Free-Vector-Images. (n.d.). *Hieroglyph Horus Egypt* [Image]. Pixabay. https://pixabay.com/vectors/hieroglyph-horus-egypt-pharaoh-33973/

Clker-Free-Vector-Images. (n.d.). *Isis Goddess Egypt* [Image]. Pixabay. https://pixabay.com/vectors/isis-goddess-egypt-egyptian-33961/

Clker-Free-Vector-Images. (n.d.). *Bast Heiroglyph Animal* [Image]. Pixabay. https://pixabay.com/vectors/bast-heiroglyph-egypt-cat-goddess-33972/

Clker-Free-Vector-Images. (n.d.). *Thoth Hieroglyph Egypt* [Image]. Pixabay. https://pixabay.com/vectors/thoth-hieroglyph-egypt-moon-god-33969/

Clker-Free-Vector-Images. (n.d.). *Anubis Jackal-Headed God* [Image]. Pixabay. https://pixabay.com/vectors/anubis-jackal-headed-god-egyptian-33974/

Printed in Great Britain
by Amazon

037eeac9-db47-46e1-a36c-671a9491fc58R01